Pastiche of Poetry

VOLUME I

A - M

50 YEARS OF POEMS
ARRANGED ALPHABETICALLY

ROSE KLIX

Address author inquiries and mail orders to:
Custom Writing Services
P.O. Box 5266
Johnson City, TN 37602-5266
Website: http://www.RoseKlix.com

ISBN-13: 978-1477490105
ISBN-10: 1477490108
Library of Congress Control Number: 2012922197
Createspace Independent Publishing Platform
North Charleston, South Carolina

Dedications

I gratefully dedicate this two-volume collection of poetry to my family, friends, instructors, poetry judges, editors, peers, and writing mentors who showered me with many discussions of my babblings. Without their assistance and encouragement, this collection would not exist. Many, many people in several locations influenced the character of my words. I list them in the Acknowledgements section of Volume II.

My family were key teachers. My mother, **Evelyn Rose,** expressed her art through quilting and oil painting. She encouraged my writing when we collaborated on quilting books. She warned, "You won't make money on poetry." Oh, well, I love it any way. My military father, **Harmon Rose**, instilled discipline within me and a critical eye. My brother **Jim** challenged me to open my mind to unusual ideas. Though they have all passed on, we will always be The Four Roses.

Thankfully, God answered my prayers and led me to my supportive husband, **Rob**. He often allows me the time and space to pursue the craft of writing. He and my precious son **Scott Anderson** and daughter-in-law **Kimberly** don't fully understand verse, but perhaps acknowledge poetry as one validation of my personality.

Sydney Martin, my best friend in Johnson City, Tennessee, always makes me feel special as we share life interests. She supported my health issue choices and challenges when I experienced breast cancer and tolerates my *airy fairy* personality. God also blessed me with enduring Rapid City, South Dakota childhood friends **Mary Butz** and **Carol Broderick**.

My neighbors **Marie Cleek**, **Doris Sanders**, and **Mary Bennett** are supportive fans. I am grateful for the times we worked together for the benefit of our condo association.

The special friends were those who shared my interest in writing. We gathered through various writers' organizations in several states. I list them all by location in the Acknowledgements section in the back of Volume II.

I particularly dedicate this collection to the variety of poets I enjoyed meeting 2010-2012 during my term as president of the Poetry Society of Tennessee – Northeast branch (PST-NE). I'm especially honored to be counted as one of the *original seven* charter members along with: **Todd Bailey, Jim Collier, Ben Dugger, Janice Hornburg, Marlene Simpson,** and **John Summers.** In 2010, more charter members joined: **Martha Culp, John Jenkins, Saundra Kelley, Ethan McCasland, Gretchen McCroskey, J. Michael Ramey,** and **Eileen Spears.** As word spread, additional poets joined us: **Tamara Baxter, Dee Bowlin, Nancy Fisher, Sharon Mishler Fox, Jo Anne Jones, Jan Mann, Sherril Miller, Chrissie Anderson Peters, David Shields,** and **Hugh Webb.** Many are taking state and national awards and publishing their poetry. I'm so proud to know them and grateful for our shared poetry times together.

I love you all!

Rose Klix

Foreword

Evening was approaching as Calliope, the poetry Muse, enjoyed a walk through her lavish garden admiring and inspiring her floribunda. Her garden sprouted plants of all sorts, but roses were her most treasured possessions. This evening, Calliope, well studied in botany, came upon a very young Rose in bud. "Ah," she said, "a Joseph's Coat Rose. Of all, these are my favorite. I will visit and nurture this one often fore as she grows she will dazzle many with her vibrancy."

And so it happened, as it was destined, from a very young age to maturity, this poet bloomed. As poetry graced her spirit, Rose met life and literary challenges with intriguing style, variety and beauty. She was rewarded with many prize winning poems, and afforded the honorable title Poet Laureate for the Poetry Society of Tennessee in 2010 through 2011.

Pastiche of Poetry displays the collected blossoms of Rose Klix's life work to date. Come, join Calliope in her garden and enjoy the poetry of her Joseph's Coat Rose.

— Marlene Simpson,
verse author of the photo book *Field of Verse*
http://www.blurb.com/bookstore/detail/2263776

Preface

Pastiche of Poetry, is a two-volume collection of poems written from
1962 through 2012. It's a hodgepodge of poems, some of which were acknowledged by awards or previous publication.

The titles in this collection are arranged alphabetically with A-M in Volume I. Those titled N-Z are in Volume II.

For anyone curious about the date order when the poems were created, I include a chronological listing in the back of Volume II, as well as a theme concordance.

This potpourri represents my efforts of emulating other poets, forms, and practicing poetry for the past fifty years. I decided to compile all of my poetry so that the whole mishmash will live together in one collection: the immature words and ideas of a teenager with the more mature mid-life writing. My voice changed over the years. Hopefully, the poetry reflects artistic growth. The simplistic and concise messages sit beside long prose-like narratives. My religious poetry are contrasted with those spiritually inspired. The pensive share a section with those more playful, the stoic with the humorous, the tributes to nature with the pains of love and loss, some honor and others bemoan family.

The poems are not necessarily autobiographical, but manifest my influences, attitudes, and imagination during the time period when inspired, written and/or edited. At first I was a shy girl and I wrote to voice my inner being. I took long breaks while I experienced life challenges. I'm still using those experiences in current poetry and learning: the more painful the feeling, the better the poetry. Oh, how we suffer for our art!

Sometimes, the poem responded to a class or workshop prompt or poetry challenge. All of the influences from many poetry coaches are manifested in these poems. I include specifics about them in the Acknowledgments section of Volume II.

I tried several formal and created forms. Some are picture poems. Others are written without punctuation. I like the freedom of free verse, but respect the enduring formal masters. Perhaps, in a much calmer lifestyle I'll reflect and grow to understand myself and my world more clearly; thus triggering another era of my poetry. One day, I may grow up, find my unique voice, and fully express myself.

Supposedly, the Mayan calendar ended on December 21, 2012. To some, this signaled tragedy. My massage therapist **Shannon Gambrell** and I joked we had hoped to succeed before the world ended! I assured her she was already successful at working out my tension. Since the world, electronics, and I continued beyond the Mayan calendar, then I plan to write even more. I personally feel this era is a new beginning cycle and not a disastrous ending. Only time will tell.

I hope you find at least one enjoyable poem to remind you of your own experiences and enjoyment in this beautiful world. Thank you for sharing our poetry time together.

Adam or Atom

Creation or evolution:
does our matter really matter?
The Creator's hand began
the process whether
with a single atom or
one spectacular event
creating Adam fully
complete with all his atoms.

Cells immediately
divide and change.
There are so many men
and women, who have
mutated throughout time.
I ask, which image
is really His?

Millions of years or a day
are all the same to Him.
Whether He created an atom,
or He created Adam
still baffles us.
Does it matter?
Either way our matter
is composed of His atoms.

Written in 2008 and won 2ⁿᵈ Place and 2010 Honorable Mention in
PST Annual Mid-South Poetry Festival.
Also published in Grandmother Earth *Volume XIX*

All I Want is More Earth Time

Teton Mountains,
Adriatic Sea,
and botanical garden views
make me want more earth time.

Days grow short,
so much to do.
Time on earth is work
and survival.

God feels far away.
I want much more.
All I really need
is nearness to Him.

Posted on Poetic Asides *in 2009*

All in a Day's Work

She, well-groomed, wears a tailored suit,
dictates letter to her male secretary.

He, fakes business smile, poises pen,
anticipates finishing correspondence.

She, after attempting a pass,
holds a tissue, but refuses to cry.

He, after slapping her face, wonders
about tomorrow's employee evaluation.

*Written in 1977 for Creative Writing class at Dakota Wesleyan University
(DWU), Published 1978 in* Prairie Winds, *Volume XXVIII
and 1978 in Colleges of Mid-America's* CMA Review

Altering Currents

Gusty, a rainy winter gale rings,
tearing apart but making whole.
A discerning Holy Spirit sings
noisy wind chimes in our souls.

Hold on lest we be swooped up
into that swirling funnel cloud.
Lightning, wind, and fire hiccup
changes when trees are bowed.

Storms of earthly gain and loss
remind us of our catechism.
Tearfully, we see an object toss,
loosening holds on materialism.

Brisk bracing air cleanses
stale lungs of aromatic earth,
configures, aims, and prods us,
prepares us for new birth.

Gentle breezes, spirit soothing,
lull us into peaceful acceptance.
The Holy Spirit, always moving
penetrates us with patience.

1999 published in The Messenger
and 2005 in Faith and Spirit *chapbook*

Always and Forever

It's no wonder, even as a child,
You spoke with authority in the synagogue.
After all – The Word was at the beginning of time.

It's no wonder Your Father exclaimed,
. . . *my Son, whom I love. . . I am well pleased.*   Math 3:17 & 17:5
After all – sinless, You obeyed and died for us.

It's no wonder You could always heal illness
and command the demons.
After all – Your Father granted You control over evil forces.

It's no wonder You could calm the ferocious winds
and walk on top of water.
After all – they obey their Creator's Son.

It's no wonder You can be with us whenever two
or more gather in your name and always.
After all – You are there every communion forgiving our sins.

It's no wonder we believe You will forever be there
whenever and wherever we need You.
After all – You were at the beginning and will be at the end.

Help us wash our robes and make them white
in the blood of the Lamb, You, our Jesus.   *Rev. 7:14*
Only then may we stand before the throne
and be counted worthy of heaven.

Thanks be unto God and to the Lamb forever and ever. Amen

Published February 2003 in The Way of the Cross; *2005 in* Faith and Spirit
chapbook, and 2010 in Spiritual Reflections *anthology*

Angora Sunset

Yesterday,
meringue clouds grayed
to mirror my dark depths
clouded by the family's
disappointing headlines.

Today,
soft and fuzzy news
covers the sky with wispy
cotton candy clouds
in an aerial sea.

Glowing gold reflects
our current blue horizons.

2005 originally recorded on The Sound of Words

Angular Vision

a Tanka form

Stern sunlight orb glows.
Rays emit angled vision.
Puffy cloud shields eyes.
Angel wings cover God's face,
soften harsh judgments of humans.

Written in 2012

Annual Mammogram

Waiting
   Is
      the
         WORST.
Just tell me I have a fatal disease
and send me to enjoy my last days.

Newsreels of dead and dying relatives
play in my head. Handy
pamphlets urge regular visits.

My eighty-five-year-old mother
bragged she never had a mammogram.
My generation accepts this annual ritual.

I stare at a dozen
magazines hiding
impatient waiting room faces.

Listen. Did that nurse mean me
with that name combination
and mispronunciation?

It sounded like Mom calling her naughty child.
The insurance company insists on
filings under my full legal name.

The nurse ignores the paper cover-up
moments before maneuvering
the vise. I sacrifice one breast at a time.

She squeezes and squeezes
tighter and tighter.
I clench my jaw and try to remember:

why at thirteen
I wanted cleavage and
when my first bra was an important event.

I sit in the second waiting room,
listen for her to call, and stand
at attention at the word *sonogram*.

Did she see something?
Another room,
another paper shirt,

another technician squeezes cold goop,
rolls a scanner over and over my breast
and frowns at the computer screen.

I say, "Hopefully, it's
just an old tired nipple."
She smiles – slightly.

I wait again while the nurse decides if
I should wait yet again.
Crisply she says, "Get dressed."

She exits, shows the images to a doctor.
I wait again. Good news.
Official report to follow.

I sigh, dress, and pass the waiting room.
Don't smile, I tell myself.
I'm the lucky one – today.

2004 Written in Laura Fargas' class at the Writers' Center in Bethesda, Maryland

Appearances

People see You less these days, Jesus.
They don't talk about Your appearances.
Are they afraid no one will believe them?

When You appeared to your disciples,
they weren't convinced You returned.
You struck Paul blind before he saw You.

Daily noise shouts at us to look elsewhere.
We know You are always there,
just below our conscious level.

We trust Your presence when we pray.
We see You every day in the children's smiles,
in kind acts, and in miraculous war rescues.

With patience, we feel Your love surround us.
When You take us home to heaven,
Your face will appear to us again.

2003 published in The Way of the Cross
and 2012 published in Common Ground Herald

April Fool

Today, I shall write all day.
First, I'll check my e-mails
and then write a poem.
Afterwards, I shall work on
my creative nonfiction essay.
The novel also needs my attention.

Oh, dear, look at all these e-mails
I must answer and forward.
I am interested in what he has to say.
She always adds a smile to my day.
This is taking too, too much time.

There it is: the poetry prompt.
Mmm. Good example. Poets already started
submitting their works for this month's
Poem-a-Day. What did they write?
Oh dear, oh dear. Lunch time and I haven't
written a single word except e-mail responses.
After eating, I will write.

I asked my husband to make a phone call
and show him the phonebook listing.
He previews what he plans to say.
The number's been disconnected.
He sits numb, unable to proceed.
I point to 23 listings in the yellow pages.
Which one, which one will he call?
I don't care. He dials and talks next to my computer.
Then, he reviews what he said. I suggest
he pass the information to his assistant.
She has an answering machine.
Because the voice is male,
he's afraid to leave a message, but does.
He says, "Why couldn't she find someone in the
phone book? It was easy." He borrows my computer,
checks his e-mail, after I log on for him.
I have a headache. So, much for writing.
April Fool's Day!

Posted on Poetic Asides *in 2009*

Rose Klix

Around and Around

a Litany form

Around and around our words repeat.
Isn't this yet the fifteenth boxing round?
Around King Arthur's round table he sat.

I can't decide to go uptown or downtown.
So, I go all around the town.
In a round church the devil can't corner me.

Round mounds of sand await my digging.
Reach around the bush to pluck the huckleberry.
Many worlds abound in the round.

Are you from around these parts?
I've come around full circle.
Around and around our words repeat.

1977 Written for DWU Creative Writing class

Ars Poetica

I must be daft to ply this craft.
Often words blow away like useless chaff.

Releasing sounds, sight, and feelings within my soul,
I wonder if I ever knew poetry at all.

Poetry cries, sighs and slowly dies,
without time to think before I dip ink.

Words and dreams start the seeding,
but I must continue to learn weeding.

Alliterative slippery stones trip me.
Then I doubt knowing true poetry.

With spading, raking and sowing gold,
I prune the rules and reshape my mold.

Whether or not clever, I'll strain
to endeavor to write forever.

Without poetry, I may occasionally
float free from explaining me,

but this is my dance, a perfect chance
to express my soul's circumstance.

Published on FanStory.com *2008*

Art Weakling

Art is far weaker than Necessity. <u>Prometheus Bound</u> - Aeschylus

I've often decided
not to quit my day job,
instead of trusting my art.
I didn't want to starve.

No on-the-job training
available for poets and writers.
That's called life. Writing's not
brain surgery, or maybe it is.

Written in 2004

Avoirdupois Dining

Chic restaurant serves a midget tray.
I swallow salad and attempt to chat,
while coveting much delicious fat.
Daintiness becomes a skill most gray.

I smile at the gracious lipped diplomat.
The plump waiter signals me behind the chap.
I drip lobster butter in the gent's lap,
while trying not to imitate Missus Jack Sprat.

Enjoying the forkfuls I scooped a scrap.
I view chunks of calorie loaded pastry.
I indicate to ladle whipped cream vastly.
My husband nudges me with a tap.

He fears my emergent angioplasty.
Gulping, I swallow words overcapacity.

Written in 2009

Away from Home in Iraq

Freedoms denied, he now defends.
Desert dry thoughts he's pushed away.
With duty and death of close friends,
festive celebrations sit gray.

Camouflage feels dusty, unclean.
Holiday hug memory churns.
Christmastide waves splash red and green
ribbons of hopeful peace returns.

Care package arrives on cool day.
Pictures and fudge shared with bunkmates.
Moods shift to laughter and horse play.
God's blessings from the United States.

2009 2ⁿᵈ Place from PST December monthly contest

Baggage

Dedicated to New Beginnings *in Rapid City, South Dakota,*
a support group for the divorced and widowed

I arrived with multiple heavy suitcases,
dragging through life, stopping my hesitant steps,
and wanting no more of pursued pity.
Holding my breath, I wheezed, then sighed.

Anger overflowed the red trunk.
Disappointment packed a blue Tourister.
Nightmares weighted my green backpack.
Pain and hurt were crammed in storage boxes.

New Beginnings lightened my luggage load.
Forgotten friendship lent me a purple duffel.
Plastic totes no longer crowded my closets.
You helped me lug attic boxes to garbage bins.

Forgiveness waited in cobwebbed corners.
Love and gratitude opened an orange carry-on.
Grains of hope trickled out a small yellow briefcase.
I gulped fresh air to exhale a welcome release.

Written in 1985,
2010 2nd Place in PST Annual Mid-South Poetry Festival
and 2011 *published in* Echoes and Images

Barn Charm

What is the charm
of an old barn?
Red faded or gray.
Tear it down, you pray.

Crunch up the land.
Raise your hand.
I know you agree,
more malls to see.

Barns sit passé.
Let them decay.
all should be gone
and not standing on.

Today's purpose for old barns
remind us of rural charms.

2008 published in Barn Charm *chapbook*

Barn on a Hill

Gray barn
on a hill
overlooking
the old still.

2008 published in Barn Charm *chapbook*

Beaver Retreat

Ad says:

BEAVER RETREAT
Splendid, spacious swimming
pool ripples and gurgles.
Includes rustic log home,
tranquil reflective trees,
cattail and lily pad gardens,
seasonal migratory neighbors.
Small, sheltered, sylvan, serene
   UNDER   CONTRACT

2005 published in Schrom Hills *chapbook*

Beginning to End

Set of Cinquain form

Beginning
Wishes,
damp from birth pains,
wriggle outside my thoughts,
itch to play beyond childish dreams,
exist.

Middle #1
Mother,
father, brother,
disciplined, teased, critiqued
used love's excuse to mold purpose,
nurtured.

Middle #2
Wife's job,
birthing children,
learning, living lessons,
straining against expectations,
divorce.

Middle #3
Accept,
understand me,
respect my ideas,
my friends, my space for creation,
accord.

Ending
Exist,
drain life daily,
dry thoughts deep inside me,
itching to re-live time's precious
wishes.

Written in 2011

Believe, Hope, Believe

Keep hope in your heart,
or troubles will start.

Once you see the light
life will be all right.

Though He stays above,
God is filled with love.

Pray. Always be kind.
It helps as you'll find.

If you try, you'll see,
and that's your best key . . .

Believe, hope, believe.

Written in 1966. Published in Faith and Spirit *chapbook in 2005*

Believing in Us

I clearly visualize your soul's character
when my brown eyes beam at your humanity.

Our shoulders bump. I hold my breath.
Your perfection brushes across my visions.

Musically, your words soothe my anxiety,
but distant static garbles your voice.

Balmy musk replenishes my craving,
allows me to inhale your essence.

Chafe my lips with kisses.
Caress me. Consume my infatuation.

I conjure up your presence
to fantasize you plus me.

Written in 1971

Berry Diamante

Berry,
it was too sweet.
She washed it down with ale.
Sweetly loving the baron, his
ecstatic limits and station allowed.
The heir didn't appear. She cried aloud.
Miffed at permanent barrenness.
It sweetly made her ail
her grave suite,
Bury.

1977 Written for DWU Creative Writing class

Beyond Me

I acknowledge the forces and entities
higher than my power and knowledge.
God inspires me to communicate
my highest good, to release any pain,
and openly express my heartfelt joys.
His inspiration mobilizes my thoughts
to heal, to comfort, to laugh, to love,
to reach out to others, who want to know
if someone – anyone – will ever understand.
I ask Him to be present with me throughout
our creative explorations together.
Amen

Written in 2012 as an invocation

Bicycle

Bicycle
exhilarating, stimulating
peddling in a verdant park
Fun

1977 Written for DWU Creative Writing class

Big Rock Candy Mountain

Grand Canyon
was just a hole.
Four Corners
empowered me
to stand in four states
at once, but
we were nowhere
breathing desert air.

Backseat napping
passed dull hours.
As a lonely teenager,
I thought my parents'
vacation boring.
I awoke to hear Dad
sing his memory of
"Big Rock Candy Mountain."

I couldn't miss seeing
that huge geologic wonder.
We stopped at a country store,
where a coyote pet was tethered.
Of course, they sold rock candy.
Syrupy sweet, but for me,
a nice family memory.

Written in 2009

Billy Collins,
Why He's My Favorite Poet

Clear, literate,
he deserved laureate title.

Irritated his neighbor's dog
barked with symphony,
he established why
his keeping gun unadvisable.*

He states poetical
anthologies encompass.
Poems need to be free,
not tortured.**

Two favorite Billy Collins poems
* Another Reason Why I Don't Keep a Gun in the House
** Introduction to Poetry

Published on FanStory.com 2008

Black Crow

a Haiku form

Black crow nods at me,
practices his prancing feet.
Feel nature's rhythms.

Written in 2005, 2012 published in Grandmother Earth Volume XVIII

Blue

Blue, my symbol
for truth and understanding.
It faded into blue smoke
and grayed my horizons.
That day I knew you were
with her.

*2010 Written in Gretchen McCroskey's Creative Writing class
at Northeast State Community College (NeSCC)*

Blue Eyes

I dig guys
with big blue eyes.
Big blue eyes
dig me.

Written in 1971

Blue Ridge Horizon

a Tricu form

Horizon
Emotionally
Expansive

Published on FanStory.com in 2008

Body, Spirit, and Thought

My body, twisted,
bent, bruised with life,
is solid but not firm.

My spirit is vaporous,
flexible, moldable, and
relearns gravity's restrictions.

My soul has been twisted,
bent, bruised with many lives,
yet remains solid with convictions.

My aura's colors deepen
with each action, reaction,
and interaction.

My thoughts are twisted,
bent, bruised by life teachers.
My comprehension fogs.

My vapor, my energy,
my light all reflect
my daily experiences:

blue ideas,
green feelings,
red emotions.

I am what I think.
I receive what I request.
I forget how to ask.

My rainbow is not
better nor less. My light
is as beautiful as yours.

Written in 2011

Boredom

Boredom
tedious, tiresome,
yawning, sleeping, droning
Fort Meade, Maryland

Written in 1993

Boxed In

Dedicated to my mother Evelyn Mae (Swinehart) Rose
October 13, 1923 to January 28, 2009

Seldom opening a crevice,
afraid of gaping unprotected,
her container often worked
safer resting horizontally,
reflecting on life, avoiding
vertical daily living.

Where do I begin
to open a rusting puzzle?
What treasures were
sequestered inside?
Vaporous spiritual
ingredients float within.

Grasp gently. Don't frighten
the unpracticed openness
of a soul tucked inside her
odd-sized earthly box.
She allowed very few
to glimpse her entirety.

Written in 2009

Boxes

I can't walk past a box
in a department store
without opening it.

At fair booths, some
are secretive puzzles.
How mysterious.

My soul is in a box
which I only open up
occasionally.

Fascinating, but perhaps
I compartmentalize
too much.

Written in 2004

Brat's Rant

To my brother Jim (James Orion Rose)

Leave Me Alone.
Don't tease me,
poke me, prod me,
and call it love.
I just want you to

LEAVE ME ALONE.

But I don't want you to,
not now, not here.
I carry you, bury you,
and wish to see your smile.
Today, I must

leave you alone.

Written in 2009

Bumble Bee's Song

Sweet blossoms, curl me up.
Perfume drench the air.
Sticky nectar, I love to sup.
Not chocolate? I don't care.

Honey, come to me.
Honey, please my queen.
Honey, set me free.
A drone – gee, I'm keen.

Hm-mmm, Hm-mmm, hm-Mmm

2005 published in Schrom Hills Park *chapbook*

Buoyant Extremity

The buoyant extremity
became as a talisman
to inoculate him against
the current axis of drift.
The paltry carrier
once was an eclipse
to a resonant paradox.
He will unlearn the change
his clan used as a carrion.

Published on FanStory.com *2008.*
The prompt required the use of certain words.

Pastiche of Poetry

Busybody

She snoops and stoops
to tell it all no matter
the subject nor who it hurts.

Today, she's spreading
gossip about someone
I know well.

I told her to stop
being a busybody
and she said she's not.

So, I described a character.
She was sure who it was
and talked and talked and talked.

I laughed, because I knew
who I wrote about
was the busybody!

Posted on Poetic Asides *in 2011*

But, Who Am I?

The earth revolves,
      but I stand still.
I reach out to touch what I see,
      but there's only empty space.

      Is someone laughing?

I run down a street.
      No one is there or anywhere.
The doors all closed.
      I watch the slowly approaching sidewalk.

      It brings me home to nobody.

There's no one but me.
I matter not.
Do you know who I am?
      Tell me, so I will know.

      No one answers.

I know not where I've been,
      where I'm going, nor where I am now.
And yet I live on
      to find my purpose.

Written in 1969

Buttercup

a Senyru form

Your child inhales a
buttercup filled with pollen,
sneezes for ages.

Written in 2011

Caged

Teenage daughter to mother –

Stop it! Stop caging me in.
I want to be free.
I want to just be.

Don't protect me.
Don't restrict me.
Let me learn on my own.

Nursing home mother to middle-aged daughter –

Protect me. Stand up for me.
Don't let them restrain me.
I can be on my own with your help.

Stop it! Stop caging me in.
I want to be free.
I no longer want to be.

Written in 2009

Canning Time

a conversation between a dead mother and her aged daughter

Evelyn Mae! What a mess on this floor.
Where are the peas to shell?
No water boiling?
Is it time to plant or time to can?
I've lost track of living time.

Mom, I pulled out a robin's
nest from my dryer hose,
but don't have energy to pick it up.
I know. The floor looks terrible.
Really, it's mostly clean.

Your kitchen bubbled with
boiling pots when you taught me
to put up jars of pickles, jams,
all kinds of vegetables from
your one-acre garden plot.

These days are different.
Sometimes, Meals on Wheels
delivers peas, cold entrées,
and horrible greens. I make do
with microwave cooking.

There's plenty to read.
I watch game shows on TV,
work my crossword puzzles,
then take a long nap in my recliner.
I can't think to do anything else.

Evelyn Mae, you know,
can't never could do anything.
Just remember this:
you can live or you can die,
but you can't do both at the same time.

2009 3rd Place in Appalachian Heritage Writers Symposium
at Southwest Virginia Community College, and

published in Spring 2012, Pasque Petals, *SDSPS anthology*

Captain, Retired

He once captained ships
and docked port to port.

Now he sits on cruises
plays the shuffleboard court,

wonders where he's been.

Written in 2012

Caribbean Heartbreak

I.

Listen, I hear a weeping abandoned child.
Unfulfilled, her fractured heart anguishes
like a mourning dove by the empty feeder.

Hide her young angel soul from
steel drum beats in a devilish syncopation.
She will remember his unfaithful love rhythms.

She should swish her ruffled purple skirts,
refuse to dance to calypso or reggae,
and escape the joyous carnival revelry.

Her heart wants to smile through pain.
I want her to run an avoidance marathon.
Hopeful illusions may shatter perceived hurt.

I'm afraid the death of innocence will race
missed opportunities wanting to trip her.
Heartbreak waits on the beach with the no see 'ems.

Published on FanStory.com 2008

Caribbean Heartbreak

II.
DETERMINATION

Morning wave splashes, slaps my face.
I kick at surf. What of my fate?
I am not whole. I am disgrace.
Pools of footprints to contemplate:
I loved. I trusted. I am lost.
He's so superior, admits no fault.
Why, oh, why must I bear the cost?
Ebbing and flowing, I call, *Halt!*
My baby stirs within my womb.
He shall never feel its flutter.
Nor will he hear my father fume.
We won't stay. I'll clear our clutter.
I kick surf, fist-shake the horizon,
clear my head to jog sand-caked toes.
Baby trusts my womb salvation.
Success? Only Creator knows.

Published on FanStory.com *in 2008*

Caribbean Heartbreak
III.
CHILD LEFT BEHIND

My son's lonely cries
rise above my lost youth.
I ask, *What if he dies?*
Then, *What if he doesn't?*

His disease diagnosed
is a tie to his father.
A child, not his boast,
openly will shame him.

Such festival, such a time,
we expressed our regrets
for our crossed border grime.
I know we share blame.

What will your wife say
to me, to our sick son?
Only his medical to pay,
will you deny and lie?

Traveling to the U. S.,
I want nothing from you.
But help your son. I guess
we'll be chained forever.

Think before you speak,
and lie on island beach.
Night's pleasure turned bleak,
affecting all us involved.

Published on FanStory.com *2009*

Charley Visits Florida

After sixty winters in Colorado, a sunshine state seduced them.
George and Louise chose a gray and wrinkled trailer court.
Their new home rejected unnecessary accumulation,
invited them to settle themselves on a warm patio.

News blared warnings of another tropical storm.
Bonnie blew through south of them yesterday.
Community postponed cribbage. Charley planned a visit.
Horseshoe pitching canceled. Neighborhood storm talk ringed.

Evacuate? They just arrived. Go where? Their son
seemed closer when they moved, but DC was far away.
George's bridge phobia, a jammed exodus, they decided to stay.
Louise recalled Midwestern blizzards, survival, and her faith.

Their Rocky Mountains wouldn't put up with Storm Charley.
The Atlantic Ocean spawned this devil. Flat land stops no storm.
Satellite imagery showed a mass whirling over the entire state.
Charley wasn't retiring, but was playing a cruel game.

Patio boxes disappeared in thick air. Walls wobbled and wafted.
Cherished china crashed. Windows spit spider web shards.
Shrubbery plopped on a sofa. Aluminum sides crinkled and cracked.
Curious Charley threw their roof across streets and peeked inside.

The couple laid under Louise's quilted Jacob's Ladder pattern.
Their kiss smacked in silence of the storm's eye. Roar built again.
George turned off his hearing aid. Louise prayed the Lord's Prayer.
Bed vibrated. Mattress climbed a wall, thumped them on the floor.

It toppled over them. Rose-patterned wallpaper pushed closer.
Dressers danced across the room. Closet emptied hangers of clothes.
They clasped hands, squeezed their eyes tight shut.
Florida held its breath. Did they dare . . . could they move?

George nudged Louise. She opened her eyes and saw his smile.
Then air raid siren split the still air. They rubbed their bruises
and thanked God. Rubbish replaced their home and possessions.
Still they laughed, imagined jumping their old bones up and down.

Emergency crew found them sorting shredded remains.
They called their son Charley from an officer's cell phone.
George told him what a rude visitor his namesake had been.
Their son hadn't visited yet, but now he was coming.

That was August 2004 when Tropical Storm Charley
visited Florida on the heels of Tropical Storm Bonnie
and before the threats of Tropical Storms Ivan and Jeanne
and maybe even more. Hurricane season wasn't over yet.

Written in 2004

Chartreuse Truce

Note: Both yellow and green liqueurs originated at Grande Chartreuse Monastery in Chartreuse Mountains of Eastern France

Elixir for long life,
a popular monastery
medicine formula.

Chartreuse,
a recipe for
herbal liqueur,

exactly fifty percent
yellow and green
competing colors.

Chlorophyll green
flavor extracted from
one-hundred-thirty plants.

Saffron produced
sweeter yellow liqueur,
reduced proof.

Carthusian monks
hid recipes. Order
politically expelled.

French government
confiscated
distillery property.

Imitators' attempts
failed. Sales poor.
Bankruptcy projected.

Monastery restored.
Production successful.
Recipes remained secret.

A nice sipping
chartreuse produced
a sweet truce.

Posted on Poetic Asides *in 2009*

Chianti

My new feisty little pet
begged an appropriate name.
Her mother answered to
Merlot named for fine wine.

Burgundy rang strong and thick.
Lambrusco murmured too masculine.
Rose' sounded pink and dainty.
Chardonnay clinked too, too long.

My puppy howled and cried.
So I named the red min-pin*
Chianti, because all the way
home I heard her sharp whine.

Miniature Pinscher Dog

Written in 2008

Childbirth Waits

an Epigram form

Childbirth waits.
Human patience grates.
Heartfelt prayer ingratiates.
Death waits.

Written in 2011

Childhood Memory

A foot-high stuffed elephant and baby doll,
cherished memories of my childhood.

My elephant has a worn spot on his trunk
from being grabbed and dragged.

My doll wears no clothes, lost
with her bottle somewhere in the years.

I love them just the same
in my personal memorial place.

I think of my elephant's comfort every time I cry.
I learned from my doll's neglect and dress my baby.

I wonder, my child, as I rock you to sleep,
I wonder what you will always remember.

Written in 1975

Christmas in Hawaii

Hawaiians strum their ukuleles
and sing *Winter Wonderland*
at the neighborhood luau.
Sleigh bells ring? Not here.

Surf's up. Watch the balancing on waves.
Warm and dry on Oahu we're happy
for a sunny walk at Waikiki Beach.
I smell like coconut from lathered lotion.

Poinsettias blossom in six-foot bushes.
On Big Island, sulfur burns noses.
Kilauea night tour lava-flow glows red.
I slip, but don't fall off the cliff.

Lush foliage frames waterfall.
Bumper sticker at Volcano House
proclaims another crappy day in paradise.
I dread flight home to fifty-degrees-below-zero.

Written in 1989

Christmas Time Again

Snow softly lands,
Salvation Army bells ring,
green and red everywhere,
decorations dangling from

spruce and pine bough scents,
poinsettias and candlelight,
caroling with church choirs,
Christmas letters mailed,

turkeys and ham roasting,
sugar cookies, mincemeat pies,
families planning their gathering,
sales and sales and sales.

My husband's tight wallet
says, "Women love to shop.
Christmas presents
are a female invention."

"No," I counter "Those
Three Wise *Men*
began the gift giving.
Santa Claus shares the blame."

Written in 2010

Church and God

A lot of bad people
attend church.
A lot of good people
search for God.

Written in 2004

Cicada Blues

Si – Si – Cicadas,
climbing up my tree.
Si – Si – Cicadas,
flying while you're free.
Si – Si – Cicadas,
Please don't land on me.

Si – Si – Cicadas,
buzzing to your mate.
Si – Si – Cicadas,
making your life date.
Si – Si – Cicadas.
breed before too late.

Si – Si – Cicadas,
dying in huge herds.
Si – Si – Cicadas,
feeding all the birds.
Si – Si – Cicadas,
you intrigue us nerds.

Si – Si – Cicadas,
deafening my ears.
Si – Si – Cicadas,
leaving without my tears.
Si – Si – Cicadas,
seventeen long years.

June 2004 Published in Greenbelt News, *during Maryland's 17-year visitation of the periodic cicadas, and 2005 recorded on* The Sound of Words

Cinnamon

I.

My dog romps in the cold,
wags an orange curly tail.
Her black nose sniffs crisp air
and exhales frosty appreciation.

Written in 2002

Cinnamon

II.

Not even knee-high,
you would fight
to the death for me.

Black streaks
enriched your
reddish gold coat.

With barks of disapproval,
your spicy personality
protected my world.

You knew my mistaken
male choices.
Finally I listened.

With your friendly
endorsement, I realized
he was our right one.

Now you are gone.
He stays and comforts me.
Thank you, Cinnamon.

We miss you.

Written in 2009

Cinnamon
III.

Dedicated to Lady Cinnamon Bear,
my best canine friend: January 13, 1992 – January 12, 2005

My spicy orange-and-black Pomeranian
liked no one, but loved my husband and me.
Her goal was not to be the pick of the litter.

Her preference was a solitary corner of the couch.
She tolerated the moves from Midwest to the
Mediterranean then the Mid-Atlantic state.

She chased sheep in the Cretan backyard
and pigeons in San Marco square, she preferred
her kennel's cool metal floor. She loved walking

and sniffing in Shrom Hills, a Maryland park.
With incessant barking, she greeted visitors,
always on guard to protect us at peril of her life.

TV program doorbells required watch-dog barks.
Nightly, for tricks and treats she performed
her repertoire of roll-over, sit, stand and dance.

Never wanting offspring she resisted
breeding efforts and ignored her one puppy.
I love you, Cinnamon, my independent feminist.

Posted on Poetic Asides *in 2009*

Cinnamon
IV.

a Haiku form

My old Cinnamon,
cold winter earth swallowed
our warm memories.

Written in 2005

Classy Scarecrows

Scarecrows* are
so fashionable today.
They're no longer
straw-headed in
flannel shirts,

But mannequins
in bright
island garb
with sunhats,
and cool shades.

Sooo, scary. Right crows?

2008 published in Barn Charm *chapbook*

* These scarecrows are a family of mannequins
in a home garden. They are seen dressed in many costumes
according to the season on Boones Creek Road in Johnson City, Tennessee.

Clean Break from Assisted Living

Mom, where are your oil paintings
and handmade quilts?
Where are your crossword puzzles
and romance novels?
Were our family pictures
moved from your bookshelf?
Was your trash emptied
of foul smelling pull-ups?
Did maintenance re-paint
your green room to institutional tan?
Did housekeeping vacuum and
shampoo for the new resident?
Will he monitor your birdfeeder
for each species' visit?
Or will she make fewer ripples
and get more attention?
Will he choose supper to be more than
mashed potatoes and ice cream?
Will she pull the emergency cord when lonely
or impatient for the bed to be made?
Will the new tenant also be moved
to the health unit to die alone?

2011 2ⁿᵈ Place in PST 54ᵗʰ Annual Mid-South Poetry Festival

Clouds

a Tanka form

Clouds translucently
clutter the wintertime sky.
Sun warms frigid lands
dissolving frozen meringue.
Mushy snow melts. Cold whispers.

*2008 Honorable Mention 51st PST Mid-South Festival
and published in* Tennessee Voices *2008-2009*

Cloudy

Wispy hints of snow banks
stretch pewter skies, gray fog
drizzles Appalachian peaks.

God-energy molds moist air
into creative shapes of galloping
steeds and nervous rabbits, or

forms polka dots on baby blue skies
to melt candy pink when farewell
sunlight borrows rainbow palettes.

God exhales and disperses clouded thoughts
which filled my apprehension. He knows:
sometimes one cloud covers my whole sky.

Written in 2008, 2011 Honorable Mention PST January Monthly Contest

Collaboration with Calliope

Calliope, of course, you sang
perfect lines of time interminable.
Yawn. But later when I'm awake.

Yes, I promised to stow pen,
flashlight, and pad under my bed.
I agreed to capture each thought.

I stumble awake, find pencil
and journal, scratch my head.
Um, birds, something, and wars?

I wasn't prepared. I valued rest.
Please whisper the verse again.
Your flawless epic dissolved.

Written in 2005

Columbus Street

Rapid City, South Dakota

Whizzing by, my childhood home looked
similar to when my parents sold it.
Dad previously pleased Mom
by painting it cyan blue in a block filled
with approved antique white.
After his experience with ladders
and short lasting paint, Dad ordered
installation of common white vinyl siding.

Rapid City leaders had demanded
property owners to pour sidewalks,
including both sides of our corner lot.
Afterwards, the chain-link fence
corralled the honeysuckle and lilac hedge,
and all provided privacy from walkers.

I had followed my brother and friends to jump
from the porch over Spirea bushes and
sprained my tailbone sliding in the grass.
The neighborhood kids had disappeared,
so have the bushes with their minute clusters
of white bridal bouquets, I had pretended
to hold against my future wedding gown.

I never forgave my parents for enclosing
their porch and removing *my* pillars.
Broken boards on the steps leaned west.
I slowed down to peer in the backyard
at the tall walnut tree. Its offspring did not survive
for Dad's planned hammock. Steel poles remain
cemented in the ground, but vacant of my swing.
Time buried Dad's horseshoe pit and strawberry patch.

I could not explore the inside that day,
said goodbye to my childhood,
and returned to my father's hospital bed.

Written in 2010 to a Creative Writing class prompt at NeSCC

Comfort

A comfort used to be Mother's kiss goodnight.
A tear on my pillow would draw her near.

It used to be a security blanket.
It was sleeping with my favorite doll.

What is it now? A locked door? A Bible?
Or a burning light? What do I use now?

An illuminated tree, a moving curtain,
a crackling furnace, and creaking furniture,

they seem so evil when I'm alone at night.
What or who will comfort me now?

Written in 1968

Communicate

I can read
upside down,
backwards
and break codes,
but I can't
read your
crossed arms
curled toes,
snide glances.
Tell me plain.
Hire an interpreter.
OMG
What's wrong?

Written in 2005

Comparisons

My grandparents, Jennie and Orion Swinehart

Jennie:
Sweet, patient
enduring,
quiet, shy

Orion:
Impatient, talkative,
swearing,
everyone's friend

Written in 2004

Complicated or Plain

Whether complicated or plain,
each quilt is worthwhile sewing.
Pieces are cut and sewn with love.
Generations built traditions.
Future quilters continue with new
innovations to keep quilting alive.

Written in 1985 for Adventures in Quilting

Compliments

He compliments me,
words I like to hear,
        not clever insight,
but pure Con-artistry.

1977 Written for DWU Creative Writing class

Conception

. . . all come from dust, and to dust all return. Ecclesiastes 3:20

I.

I'm a dust speck. No, I am not dust.
I feel empty and alone in a dark void.
No one can look at me. I listen to the lowest piano tone,
a gruff, joyless A playing seven times.
Hope climbs the keys one-half step at a time. I resonate
and inhale deeply, humming a Middle C pitch, a long breathy *ooh*.
A hoarse shadow expresses, *Free Will*. Softly, I chant,
I am aware of my choices.
My vibrations ripple to earth. Crimson spirals deep in my base.

II.

I feel warmth. I feel peace. I feel love. Who is in my consciousness?
I open my truthful eye. An indigo blue mist envelops me.
Jesus, in my favorite azure cloak, hugs me! Tears pool on my smile.
Pasque flower sachets sprinkle over me. I taste chocolate mints.
White wings blur past. I hear whispered gentle breezes,
Cleanse your past. May I learn more life purposes?
Forgive us, other souls smile. *Forgive me.* I chant, *I am aware of
my intentions.*
Together we souls hum a long O at a Middle D pitch.
Orange spirals in my abdomen.

III.

Maybe I am stardust. I sparkle so slightly, twinkle, pulse,
and reflect the universe.
An arpeggio flows up the piano keys
and quivers on the very last C tone.
The keys trickle down faster, then brighter to Middle C.
There is a spark.
Two octaves higher C, D, C tones trill.
Two octaves lower another simultaneous trill.
All celestial keys cascade to Middle E.
We hum this pitched *ah,* exhaling all breath.
I hear, *Thoughts create.* Fractionated cells,
a glimmer, a passion, and I'm conceived.
Now I exist again.
Shhh. Did I hear a heartbeat shudder?
Yellow spirals in my center.

2008 selected as the on-line Reader's Choice Award sponsored by
Voice Magazine for Women *and published in their August 2008 print edition,*
also in 2008 published in The Collection of Mid-South Poetry Festival
for PST

Contemplation

Floating through space without a problem
would be wonderful, but not quite heavenly.

It would be nice for an hour, or even a day,
quiet and serene, just me and my dreams.

It would be lonely and boring up there by myself.
My thoughts would be back here with you.

I'd miss you. Would you miss me?

Written in 1972

Contrasts

Majestic!
My heart swelled while I stared
at the grandiose mountains of Utah.

Yuk!
Garbage floated in an aquarium tank.
This demonstration of pollution repulsed me.

Angry at seeing such desecration paired with nature
sickened me, momentarily spoiled our trip.

1977 Written for DWU Creative Writing class

Cottontail Challenge

Hop an unpaved trail,
dodge kids with dogs,
forage food,
scratch ticks or fleas,
be alert from dawn to midnight,
bunk in rain-soaked thickets,
design a nest alone,
wiggle your nose,
turn your ears,
listen to noisy birds,
never complain out loud,
master the cottontail challenge.

2005 published in Schrom Hills Park *chapbook*

Couldn't a Snake Giggle?

Couldn't a snake giggle
wherever he'd wiggle?

Couldn't a frog grin
before he'd jump in?

Couldn't a dog smile
for a little while?

Wouldn't it be dull
not to laugh at all?

Couldn't a pig sigh
when ready to cry?

Couldn't a cow pout
when really put out?

Couldn't a horse frown
on a day he's down?

Wouldn't it be hard
not to express a word?

A squirrel will chatter.
So, what's the matter?

Horses neigh, lions roar,
pigs oink. I needn't say more.

1989 1ˢᵗ Place at Central States Fair, Rapid City, South Dakota

Cozy at Last

Redbud trees bloom on the hill.
Our new rose bushes sprout red points.
Forsythias blossom against the woods
by the sticker bush. The cardinal guards
his birdfeeder hanging in the spruce tree.
This spring I'm cozy in my condo
where we enjoy natural views at long last.

Posted on Poetic Asides *in 2011*

Crazy Eddie, One Unfortunate Veteran

An anesthetized eddy, a clogged cesspool,
refuses to drain more than a drop at a time.
He allows only the clear and true to dissipate,
hates to be stuffed full of potential.

He denies the existence of hopeful expressions.
Pessimism clouds his already darkened tunnel.
His un-lauded martyrdom beats its breast
and inaudibly exclaims to numbed ears.

Income and outflow – he drinks to forget –
but never forgets to drink to remember,
reminding everyone of the disregarded adjudications.
Alcohol became the reality he drinks to flush away.

Balancing the ups and downs keeps him unbalanced.
Beer teeters less predictable peaks and valleys.
His productive existence has been effectively
paralyzed in a septic tank of unexpressed rage.

Excuses puddle up, choke sympathy, because
no one wants to hear the details. His muddied mind
grasps the negative. Sufficient enablers get just enough
to disappoint them. Blame is everywhere and nowhere.

Allowing only the clear and true to dissipate,
he refuses to drain more than a drop at a time,
remains a clogged cesspool, an anesthetized eddy.
He wears his only allowed badge, that of a damaged war vet.

1989 1st Place Central States Fair, Rapid City, South Dakota

Crazy Poetry

a Villanelle form

Mad for this crazy poetry,
my life's favorite slow dance
includes words which explain me.

I tire from helping you to see
my weird circumstance.
I'm mad for crazy poetry.

Please, I beg you, just let it be.
Don't try the clever enhance
nor include words to explain me.

I suppose you would agree,
without reason perchance,
I go crazy mad for poetry.

There is no written guarantee
you'd forego a second glance
to include words which explain me.

Go away. I'll clear out our debris.
I hate to take this drastic stance.
Crazy me remains mad with poetry,
because it includes words to explain me.

Written in 2011

Crimson Smudge

A crimson smudge quivered on hot pavement,
trickled into the ditch, fed the thirsty grass.
A smudge of guts and gore lay exposed on the road.
God's creation ceased to exist except in imagination.

Squashed cells had been built and modified
into a possum, a rabbit . . .maybe a favorite pet.
Hurrying tires barely felt a small bump before
the crimson smudge quivered on hot pavement.

1977 Written for DWU Creative Writing class

Cross Country Ski Lesson

I stood on wooden planks
and faced the instructor.

My plan:
take lessons,
avoid the declines
and inclines,
stay on even ground.

I didn't want to slip
and slide into trees,
nose dive into snow banks,
or tangle poles and skis.

Her plan:
First, you must fall down.
Tip over. Lie in the snow.
Kick your skis up.
Find your footing.

Fall down? Facing the instructor,
I stood on wooden planks.

2010 Written in Creative Writing class at NeSCC

Crossing the Street

My street becomes a highway, a raceway.
Young drivers ignore all posted speed signs.
School bus slows traffic with inpatient lines.
I would stop them all if I had my way.
Traffic flows as fast as Bristol Speedway.
Police should patrol and give out stiff fines.

Neighbors open doors for roaming canines,
who wander around whether night or day.
Screech. Smack. I hear awful sounding whines.
Guilty vehicle speeds away doesn't slow down.
Dog cries out and crawls. Owner crosses lane,
bundles up his best friend, speeds to the vet.

When will this county become a real town,
where a loose dog won't be a triathlete?

Written in 2009

Cruising

Baltimore, Maryland to Newfoundland, Canada

You promised me
fall colored ports of call
at Baltimore, Boston, and Portland.

You assured me gold and
crimson New England scenery
spilled into St. John and Halifax.

Remnants of tropical storm Erika
and Atlantic Ocean waves
fiercely rocked our beds.

The first full day,
I saw vanilla stateroom walls
and a pink trash bucket

where I suffered seasickness worse
than any flu. Moving TV pictures were
intolerable in unsettled water.

I missed the first formal dinner
and did not care to shop or view
Las Vegas style entertainment.

My queasy husband reported
crew members taped paper bags
along hallways and on stairway railings.

Misery loves company.
We were all in the same boat!

Written in 2010

Crystal Rose

I am a crystalized rose,
frozen in time.
You think me
rigid, unfeeling.
Crystals breathe.
No one measured
my fractions of growth
in their lifetime.
Occlusions appear
to be fault lines.
I desire to teach
secrets of centuries.
Learn my lessons.
Handle carefully.
Don't place me
on a shelf you
forget to dust before
Grandma visits.

Written in 2004

Dad's Hats

in memory of my father Harmon Lee Rose 1919 to 2001

Dad's National Guard
khaki-green work hat
protected his bald head.

On Sundays, his dress hat,
tan with a wide band,
sat at attention in the pew.

His mechanic's hat, covered
with greasy mind-scratches,
helped to extend our car's life.

Dad's hat always touched
his heart for the parade flag or
during the national anthem.

He wore his VFW uniform hat
when his rifle fired many
twenty-one gun salutes.

Outdoors, I rarely saw Dad
without his hat. One day his comrades
removed their hats to salute his grave.

Written in 2010

Dad's Razor Strop

Dad displayed his proud
rummage sale find.
He snapped the leather strap
to illustrate his power.

I buried the razor strop deep
in the ghost's closet under
the extra sheets and towels.
Cowhide and metal wouldn't hit me.

When asked, I feigned
ignorance and shrugged.
So what, if it was misplaced?
It stayed away from me.

Maybe it surfaced during
their move to retirement living.
I don't care where it is.
I exerted my power.

Written in 2010

Daughter of Selu*

I am immature, innocent,
sweet and shy green corn.
At first harvest, I want to be
savored and to satisfy you.

Free me from my leafy wrapping.
I give you each tasty kernel.
Enjoy me before crows peck my spine
or beetles crawl across my perfection.

I'm still bound to my mother creator,
not liberated nor independent, and yet
ripening rapidly, releasing pollen, begging
for fertilization, afraid to be overripe.

My tender love may not survive
your plucking my maidenhead, but
don't leave me to rot on the stalk
like an old maid, plowed under, unfulfilled.

Selu = Cherokee Corn Mother

*2011 White Buffalo Native American Poet Laureate Peace Pipe Award
and publication in* Gifts of the Great Spirit, Volume II

Day Before Christmas

The day before Christmas
all through the room
went a tremendous boom.
It sounded like thunder.
By Jove, I wonder,
could he have come early this year?

There was a crash on the rooftop
My broom fell from my hands, ker-plop.
I looked out and saw her glide.
Down the awning she did slide.
With a hop she was at the door
by now, *I* was on the floor.

She rapped on the knocker
and this is the shocker.
It was all a big funny.
There stood the Easter bunny.

Written in 1967

Day Has a Trillion Eyes

Original: The Night Has a Thousand Eyes by Francis William Bourdillon 1852-1921

The day has a trillion eyes.
Right, not only one.
Yet the bright light soon dies,
if we can't save our sun.

Conscience has a trillion eyes,
each heart beats for one.
Yet the earth of our life soon dies,
if global care is not done.

Posted on Poetic Asides *in 2009.*
The prompt directions were to change a famous poem.

Day Into Night

a Glosa form

Original lines: *The Eagle* by Alfred Lord Tennyson
He clasps the crag with crooked hands;
Close to the sun in lonely lands,
Ringed with the azure world, he stands.
The wrinkled sea beneath him crawls

He clasps the crag with crooked hands.
A silver sided fish he spies,
as sharply seen by eagle eyes.
This morning warns his piercing shriek.
Flexing curved claws, he leaves the peak.

Close to the sun in lonely lands.
Then swooping wings fly seaward bound.
With victory shrieks, he stays crowned.
He fluffs feathers, strengthens his might,
swallows the fish. He gulps one bite.

Ringed with the azure world, he stands.
A lonely mighty king, he's found.
His mate soars her smooth-feathered gown.
With sharp contrast, spies graying light,
settles to nest. Day passes to night.

The wrinkled sea beneath him crawls.
Today left no regret nor trace.
He heralds ancient time and place.
World king found his elected space.
He desires to share his home base.

Written in 2009

Dead Computer

Jumps me to life as I erase
the memory, feed it discs.
It sticks out its CD-drive tongue
and begs me to renew
the lozenge circled mind.
I am a prisoner awaiting the next step.
At least, it didn't want another trip
to the factory reset agents – this time.

2010 Written in creative writing class at NeSCC

Deadline Jack

a Senyru form

deadline-driven Jack
sped to sales lot last minute
in previous life

2011 Honorable Mention PST May Monthly Contest

Death by Identity

I became daughter,
sister, wife, and mother.
Identities smothered my unique parts,
pleased everyone, but lost myself.

I heard your dictates, but your control
stifled my true existence. Once,
I allowed your attempts to mold me
into your imagined female perfection.

My obedience hurt my self-esteem,
until I listened to my own thoughts.
When left alone, I will survive your
suffocation and revive my true identity.

Posted on Poetic Asides *2009*

Death by Love

You were not neglected.
I left you protected,
surrounded by caregivers.

I wanted you to live,
not just exist. We all
worked to encourage you.

A hard-headed Dutch woman,
Mom, you had your own ideas of life,
of how and when you would die.

Yes, it does all seem unreal.
Your medicine-induced dreams
formed a cloudier reality.

Now, I suspect you died
of self-neglect from a life
surrounded by much love.

Written in 2011

Death – Our Success

We climb up the steps and stumble on a few.
Our goal is high, but we must try to reach it.
We fight a continuous battle.
We climb up the steps and fall down.
As people, we choose to ascend or descend.
Our Guide lets us go our separate ways.
He still guides us to our central goal.

We climb up the steps and gain a few.
The staircase spirals in front of us
makes us dizzy with defeat and success.
We climb up the steps, fall, and stumble.
Our way is hard and we hurt.
But when we hit the bottom,
where we began,
we've also reached the top
where we finally meet our Guide.

Written in 1966

Designed Intelligently

A fault line runs through me,
enters my left temporal lobe,
labors to exit my great right toe.

A victim attitude created
various occlusions within my soul,
memories, bits of unresolved pains.

With scratched spectacles,
I resolve to clear my karmic residue,
imperfections all my experiences created.

Intelligent light may release soul slights.
Accepts, not a fault line, but my bent energy
becoming more grounded each decade.

Written in 2008

Detour These Dangers

Railroad crossing flashing lights,
rancid smelling meat,
high-pitched whistles,
growling, chomping bull dog jaws,
teacher's one eyebrow raised,
rattling snakes,
handling burned campfire marshmallows,
inhaling diesel exhaust fumes,
ex-spouse's threats,
hurricane winds,
scrumptious calories,
Mother's warning scowl,
downhill interstates with faulty brakes,
unprotected computer programs,
Dad's snapped leather belt,
fog horns on open sea,
and most of all,
Detour:
a wink, flirty smile, and
dancing cheek to cheek.

2010 2nd Place in PST November monthly contest

Devil in the Rain

Piercing rain spatters
my window. Footsteps
interrupt dreams.
Your insistent knock
demands I peep at your
tempting dark red hair.

With a quivering
flushed whisper,
I ask your desire.
A clap of thunder
and your voice
snaps, "You."

Loneliness hides.
My translucent heart
squeezes all
into that moment.
I recklessly open wide
to your marriage proposal.

Inside a small
familiar space,
in a white hot instant,
your lightning perforates
my saved innocence,
denies its restoration.

Wind rattles
blue window shades,
frightens my desires.
I sense impurity
in shadows
of Virgin Mary.

Lingering ghosts
of your past loves haunt
our gray corners.
Demanding you, "Go."
I watch your crimson head
shake as you stomp away.

My loneliness resurfaces.
with your transmitted disease.
While you conquer another's innocence,
I plea for return of purer fantasies.

Written in 2004 in Rose Solari's Poem-A-Day class,
at the Writers' Center in Bethesda, Maryland
Published in 2011 Howl, *a literary and art review from Virginia*
Highlands Community College, Abingdon, Virginia

Diet Moan

Diet:
salad and grapefruit,
cabbage soup.
No, not yucky carrots.

No potatoes and gravy,
or donuts and cookies,
not even milkshakes
or BBQ chips?
Moan.

It would be
easier to diet,
if I didn't have
any taste buds.

1977 Written for DWU Creative Writing class

Digitalization

Devoid of laptop,
PDA, or Wii –
my son likens me to an alien.

Scott says, "Didn't you receive
your welcome package when
you arrived on Planet Earth?"

People crowd roads and stations
but speak to others with
blue-toothed cell-phoned ears.

Digital TV required equipment update
and sucked us into dependence on
cable and satellite entertainment.

One day, I may decompose in a Star Trek
transporter. My molecules will jumble
when you must restart the machine.

Written in 2009

Discontent

I wish I were anything, but myself.
I want to be part of nature
without worries.

I could be a stream,
content to flow endlessly
with a breeze blowing gentle ripples.

I could be a tree,
stand steadfast against the sky,
stretch toward the sun and stars.

I could be a bird,
welcome each day with cheerful chirping,
free to fly among the clouds.

But if I were a stream,
rocks scrape as I flow onward.
Raindrops disturb my calm.

If I were a tree,
wind tears my branches.
Fowl and pests pierce my bark.

If I were a bird,
a storm disturbs my tranquil flight
or a young boy discovers my nest.

I shall be content to be myself.
I'll be part of your life.
We'll share our sorrow and pleasures.

Written in 1974

Discord

A giant tiger lily shot up to the window.
It grew tall and straight,
proud of itself towering above the others.

It saw the finger pointing and fist slamming,
wilted, no longer straight.
It couldn't watch the screaming and crying.

They were sad when their beautiful,
but tormented, flower died.
They blamed each other.

1977 Written for DWU Creative Writing class

Disorganization

My disorganization
is the only
organization.
What a mess!

Written in 1990

Dorothy

For my friend Dorothy Borelson 1931-2010.

I smile at your letters on recycled
greeting cards and think often of you
and your woodstove warmed farmhouse.

Thank you for the weather reports,
your latest count of hundreds
handmade quilts on your treadle machine

with donated scraps.
Lutheran World Relief
should send *you* groceries.

On hospital trips, you pushed Carol
in her wheelchair, so you
could endure cancer treatments.

Mine was the seventy-sixth card
pen pals sent for your 75th birthday.
My faithful friend, you also remembered my day.

You don't bring in the cows,
or enjoy the banty roosters now,
but still adopt stray kittens.

Snoopy barks for your scraps.
You write about the cardinal
in your feeder and never moan,

complain, fuss, or cry about
your parents dying, or discuss giving up
your life to care for your retarded sister.

Written in 2004

Dread

Dread reminds me of the DC Sniper.
We waited on the Metro platform
like innocent ducks in a barrel.
Dread is to ski downhill
without lessons or poles.
Dread is a hot air balloon when the pilot
cannot find a better landing field.
Dread is when I waited for my parents
to learn I'd broken the coffee table,
because I kicked at my big brother
to stop his perpetual teasing.
Dread is becoming the last
of my family – the four Roses –
and the knowledge
I will follow them one day.

Written in 2010 Creative Writing class, NeSCC

Dreams

Reach high, sparkle bright.
The sky's the limit.

Stretch up, stretch out.
The world is right,

because you're in it!

Written in 1968

Drifting

Drifting through
clouds, this speck
feels complete
just floating.

No mission in
mind or heart
replaces this
peacefulness.

Do souls need
a body to feel
fulfilled? What
is so important?

Should I choose
an earth existence
again? Will I find
relevance this time?

My journey starts
with siphoning me from
tranquility and being
placed inside a human shell.

Will I succeed? What is my
quest this lifetime? As I
drift closer to earth
my mission clouds.

Posted on Poetic Asides *in 2010*

Drip Drop

Two-year drought
sprinkles renew my chi.
Neighbors join
my mud dance.

We bow humbly to sky,
Welcome and bless abundance,
never enough
until it's too much.

Drip drop, rain falls.
Soggy ground, lakes, and rivers
overflow until lost at sea
as a siphon of nature's circuit.

Written in 2002

Drought

The rapidly maturing shoots
waved a welcome to warm sun.
Gentle breezes toyed with its leaves.

Knee high by the Fourth of July
would be easily possible.
Rapid progress made the stalks laugh.

Gratefully, shoulder-high corn
kissed Mother Nature's rewards, but
a little rain would be welcome.

Merciless sun burned holes
in the summer. The ground cracked
and begged for moisture and relief.

June happiness wilted into August anguish.

1989 published in Dakota Plains & Fancy
for the Vermillion, Literary Project, South Dakota

Drought's Rain

Blood of the land

dripped from the sky,
fed all the vampiric plants.

They lapped it up, used it,
let sun evaporate it,

then, begged for more.
      Gluttonous fools!

Written in 1977 in DWU Creative Writing class

Dry Leaves

a Haiku form

Crackling harvest leaves,
crunchy dry blanket hides seeds.
Green hints hibernate.

Written in 2005, 2007 Published in Lost State Voices, *Volume II*

Each One a Star

In memory of the Space Shuttle Challenger disaster and inspired by John Gillespie Magee, Jr. poem High Flight*

Stars, Stars up so high,
we'll learn from you and know,
blazed against the sky,
unsatisfying glow.

Once, one fantastic shooting star;
it was an amazing sight.
A moment, then an ugly scar,
our space shuttle burning bright.

The horizon, covered in research,
knowledge of space was in your care.
Ashes have fallen to the earth,
but your essence is everywhere.

Astronauts, astronauts up so high,
with curiosity about a star
are now part of our planet's sky.
But have you gone and reached too far?

Can you now touch the face of God?*

Written in 2003, 2007 Published in Lost State Voices, *Volume II*

Eagle

a continuation of The Eagle with apologies to Alfred Lord Tennyson

A silver sided fish he spies.
as sharply seen by eagle eyes,
used grasping strong pliers, he flies.

Then, swooping wings fly upward bound,
with victorious shrieks stays crowned,
and like a mighty king, he's found.

Written in 1985 with my explication of a poem
for the Man and His Literature *class at*
South Dakota School of Mines and Technology, Rapid City, South Dakota

Early Bird Routine

Early bird gets the worm!

Each morning you try to wake me
with enticements of your catalog
of visitors to the birdfeeders.
I hear them thanking you at dawn
and muffle their songs with my pillow.

Cardinals, doves, bluebirds,
blackbirds, a woodpecker, and robins
have all disappeared by the time
the sun is at its peak and
I appear at the window.

I've never desired to dine on worms
and neither, I believe, have you.
Although, I don't watch you
consume your birdwatcher's breakfast.
Maybe you do enjoy worm mush
stirred into your raisins and oatmeal.

Posted on Poetic Asides *2009*

Ears of Corn

Kernels of life survive
inside ears of corn.
Golden tassels
capture sunshine.

Crows spy it, peck it,
defy waving arms.
Field mice pick up
leftovers for their families.

Cherokees honor
as a third sister.
Green Corn Ceremony
pardons all infractions.

Long seasons await
edible kernels of life
to wipe the spirit clean.
Sing of *Selu, Corn Mother.*

*Written in 2009, 2012 received White Buffalo Silver Sage Award
and published in* Gifts of the Great Spirit, *Volume II*

Easier

It is easier
for some to be
mothers when they
don't have any children

*1977 Written for DWU Creative Writing class
and 1978 published in* Prairie Winds, *Volume XXVIII*

Easter at Last!

Long, cold, snowy winter,
let's skip straight to spring.
Green stems peek at me.
Clearing last year's dead leaves,
I help shake off winter blankets.
Daffodils and crocuses bud.

I want to fast forward to Easter
and celebrate Christ's shaking off death.
He triumphed. Glorious day!
Wonderful resurrection –
for Him – for humanity!
Easter lilies trumpet victory.

During Holy Week I remembered his passion,
His suffering on the cross for our sins.
When I pick up a flyer dropped at my door,
I gasp at that grotesque picture:
Jesus crucified, bleeding, lightning striking,
captioned, *All this I did for thee.*

I hate that cold vision of Christ
and caress my favorite gold cross,
which doesn't literally show His pain.
I avoid wallowing in the vision of Him dying
and push away thoughts of unnecessary suffering.
Why can't I skip straight to His victory?

During Lent I reflect, self-examine,
and remember Christ. I force myself
to look on His bloody picture, cry,
and remember how He saved me.
I thank Him for taking away my sins.
My shivering path to Easter was painful.

I hated the winter. Spring arrives sweeter.
I hated Christ's painful bleeding.
Glorious resurrection! He restored hope.
Jesus in heaven intercedes for sins.
Christ's suffering is past.
Winter is finished. Ah, Easter at last!

2003 Original version published in The Way of the Cross,
and 2012 March/April edition of Common Ground Herald

Eating Disorder

Enjoy your meal.
Don't worry about
starving thousands.

Pay no attention
to outsourced local farmers
or underpaid foreign workers.

Ignore the screams
of slaughtered animals
and castrated calves.

Soy beans aren't
really all that good
for you, are they?

Don't worry about
stinking sanitation ditches.
Enjoy your meal.

Have a cigarette, too.

Written April 2005

Editorials

a Senyru form

Editorials
give many opinions to
brew up complaining.

Written in 2009

Elusive Pen

I beat the papers on my desk
in the hope of finding my elusive pen.
I shake the papers and exclaim,
"Who stole my pen, again?"

I describe it in detail
including the tooth markings
and the worn clicker.

I crawl on the floor searching
under desks and chairs.
I stomp to the supply closet in desperation,
and grab another ink writing stick.

When I thrust my hands
into my sweater pocket, I must blush
as I produce my prize pen.

I should label it, tie a string on it,
or type with it in my hand,
but how else could I get a better
diversion from work?

Written in 1985

Embraced Love Released

Edna St. Vincent Millay *Love is not all: It is not meat nor drink*

a Ghazal form

Love's nourishment is not food, not even meat nor drink.
I survive imbibing through life, not with meat nor drink.

Across the window's curtained wink, our hope now flitters,
declining safety and our denying meat nor drink.

My heart's expected sink from footsteps creeping to wait.
Temptations grab our sighs free of neither meat nor drink.

Our safety brink is not confinement within four walls.
Affair offerings refused for more than meat nor drink.

Across a smooth frozen rink, released love skates freely.
Petrified love, a statue, never wants meat nor drink.

This rose's soul cracks. Clinks of chances remain depressed.
Embraced love nourishes, but never as meat nor drink.

2009 Written in Cathy Smith Bower's class at
Tennessee Mountain Writers Conference in Oak Ridge, Tennessee

Erik

He cried when I left.
He told me I was wrong.
He couldn't stay clean.
I miss him, especially now.
He's gone.

1977 Written for DWU Creative Writing class

Erik's Elegy

For my son Erik Lee Anderson: April 23, 1972 – December 19, 1974

Sixteen years quickly disappeared,
since I watched my curly haired cherub
somersault from the sofa, devilishly pull
our cat Patch's tail, and never listen to *No*.

God, I ache to hug him and present him
with eighteen candles this birthday.
I missed him struggling into a prom tuxedo.
He didn't graduate into adulthood years.

I still miss his bedtime sing-song chant
accompany me after our prayers.
Instead I wrote, *Jesus Loves me. Amen.*
an eternal inscription on a flat granite slab.

Lord, please give him back. One thieving
careless moment robbed my years of delight
and pride in my son. Agony replaced him.
You'll take better care of Erik, but I still love him, too.

Written April 23, 1990

Erik's Museum Elegy

I lived in a green house with a sculpted shag rug
and everything in Daddy's favorite color, with
our St. Bernard dog washing my face, and
Scott my three-year-old brother.

In the snow, neighbors Carol and Willy
brought us home from church.
Mom went outside to feed rabbits and chickens.
We stayed in the warm house
with Scott's orange medicine bottle
Momma never spooned to me.

Daddy came home for lunch,
I somersaulted off the green sofa
and giggled. Momma worried.
He saw no problem and returned
to work driving our only pick-up truck.

At naptime I choked.
Momma's eyes dripped.
She woke Scott, grabbed his hand,
and carried me next door
to borrow the neighbor's phone.
The hospital sent us to Denver
for a small enough dialysis machine.
It was Momma's first airplane ride
and my last one.

Written in 2010 from a prompt in Jane Hicks workshop
sponsored by PST-NE

Eve

First, a unique woman,
with taste for the first sin,
the first mother,
and the first who grieved
her lost child.

Written in 2012

Evelyn

Dedicated to my mother, Evelyn Mae (Swinehart) Rose
13 October 1923 to 28 January 2009

Your eightieth birthday notice
mis-headlined your celebration.
We laughed and called it a prediction.
Friends complimented you as looking
really good for a ninety-year-old.
The celebration was festive, but
clearly you looked worn out.

Widowhood was too difficult to
bear alone. You spent the next
five years in one retirement home
after another, bragging you had
tested all three levels. Independent
living wasn't independent enough.
Assisted living didn't assist enough
and the nursing home
was just a waiting room.

You envisioned a parade welcoming
you to your eternal home and
was concerned about the impatient
horses. When I visited that last day,
your puzzle pieces were clearly
missing. I truly missed your laugh,
your grumbled complaints,
your quilting expertise, and
your very own unique memories.

Posted on Poetic Asides *2009*

Ever Forever

Wye Oak Tree, Wye Mills, Maryland circa 1540-2002

Citizens cried from bay
to mountain to city.
Oh, champion Wye Oak,
for five centuries you defied
lightning, fire, and industrial progress.
As an old war general, you proudly
displayed the wires anchoring your
branches, relieving your stress.

Humans were fenced
from your tender roots.
Interventions didn't stop
the wrinkles in your
death-challenging battle with disease.
An ambassador of nature,
you won many a skirmish,
but time won its war.

A turbulent thump echoed
throughout Maryland.
Catastrophic winds
dropped your branch-tips
to the cruel pavement.
Your damaged torso
convulsed the ground.

I whined that you were gone.
With a moan, I thought, *a time comes*
for all of us to part this world.
You were our beloved state tree
and I celebrate your longevity.

Now scientists study your diseases.
Your clones are nurtured in other parks.
Each, leaf, branch and root is cataloged
and saved for someone's special artwork.

In my imagination, you will
eternally stretch your arms to touch
the sigh of each visiting cloud and
forever be our oldest wooden companion.

Written in 2004. Published in Iguana Review, *Volume #5 Summer edition 2005*

Ever Green

My whole world became
as green as the cable
sweater he wore on our first date.
In our home, we chose
a green patterned sofa
and sculpted shag carpet
pitted with splotches of green.
The outside walls surrounded
us in green wooden siding.
I'd embraced his favorite color.

I learned to hate him and
thus avoided his color anywhere.
I turned away from green
in clothing, furniture, and paint.
My reaction to his actions
deprived me of a basic color.

Crete, Greece was olive drab
and no grass poked through the gravel
except in the country where some
blades dared be near the ancient diggings.
A few dusty leaves on vegetables
survived another drab green.

Over Italy, green appreciation returned to me.
The first sight was out an airplane window.
Land and trees were forest green.
My heart raced and my eyes widened.
I don't think I could have absorbed Ireland,
just then. I couldn't wait to land.
I didn't realize how much I missed green.

I don't hate him,
any more than I hate green.
What a lovely color to bring
natural balance to my life.

2010 Written in Creative Writing class at NeSCC

Everyone Knows

God knows
everyone should know:
God knows
everyone.

2005 published in Faith and Spirit *chapbook*

Expiration Date

He died! I didn't even know him, but he died. He's dead!
He lived down the hall from us and now he's dead and gone.
Was he the man who glared while waiting for the mailman each day?
Or the gentleman who helped carry my groceries?

Apartment Number Nine – I wish I could picture his face.
Someone died here today. Someone I didn't even know.
I really wish I knew who he was that I mourn.
He died. I didn't even know him, but he died. He's dead.

1977 Written for DWU Creative Writing class

Face It

This is the ugly face
I make when I hear you shout
into the phone and guffaw loudly.

I cannot work,
I cannot think.
I close my door
over and over.
Each time it slams louder.

You said, "Didn't know
there was a problem."
You'd forgotten the first day
I said, "This was the quiet end of the suite."

I asked you to be quieter.
You said, "That is my inside voice.
Did you expect whispers?"

You ignored both me and
our colleague's requests.
Only e-mails got your attention.

This is the smiley face
I show now
we are quieter friends.

Written in 2004

Fair Enough

I inhaled a funnel cake,
blew powdered
sugar dust clouds.

Licked a cherry
snow cone, I slurped
the last sweet juice.

I sucked sticky
cotton candy
fingers clean.

Kicked at sawdust,
I avoided tripping
on electrical wires.

Scents of hot dogs
and cow manure
mixed in the air.

Who wants to hang
upside down, swing
dizzy on rides?

I'd rather overload
my tummy with
usually ignored treats.

Campbells ain't
got nothin' on these
delicate fairground staples.

Mmm, Mmm good!

Written in 2010

Fairy Wand Star

Tarnished and chipped,
I am only a loose button
looking for secure knots.

I wanted to be the star
in her fairy wand, an emblem
of every wish without blinking.

She sang,
"Star light, star bright.
I wish I and the whole world
could be very, very happy."

Maybe I should wish
I were a butterfly,
and fly away with her troubles.

2010 Written from a button bowl prompt
in a Jane Hicks workshop sponsored by PST-NE

Pastiche of Poetry

Fall Leaf Confetti

Fall leaf confetti
rained on my car,
looked like a parade decoration
blown free from a float.

2010 Inspired in the Creative Writing class at NeSCC

Families

Families are wonderful.
Families are great.
Families sit you down
to clean your plate.

Written in 2003

Family Cemetery Meeting

Pedro, South Dakota

Annually, decayed headstone decorations are refreshed.
A reunion of family members, mow, rake,
and replace plastic flowers. Three family branches
meet, argue business, and then eat.

The Iraqi war ain't got nothin'
over my family's cemetery meetings.
Maybe not from bullets and bombs,
but verbal and mental wounds damage.

The problem is an entire branch who love
discussion and debate. Our representative
stands up for her convictions. Cousin tells her
to shut-up while brandishing his revolver.

One time only two aunts attended and both
brought baked beans. When retelling this story,
Aunty sang, *Beans, beans, the musical fruit.*
Since then each brought an entire meal – just in case.

At Grandma's October funeral. The National Guard
transferred her casket into their four-wheel-drive truck.
I was a teenager and my fashionable black lacy scarf
wasn't smart protection against freezing prairie winds.

Sometimes, but thankfully not when I am there,
rattlesnakes slither across the graves planted on a one-acre
homesteaded hump of South Dakota prairie grass.
Hopefully, everyone remembers to close all four cattle gates.

We often worry if drought narrowed the Cheyenne River
and sympathize with those working this unforgiving land.
Spring rains slick clay gumbo on the hilly climb
and challenge our right turn at the poorly marked Y.

One July, Dad showed my fiancé
the cemetery where my ancestors rest.
We entertained ourselves during the fifty miles
on I-90 and fifty more on country roads.

Dad sang "Cowboy Jack" at my request.
We laughed through several verses of "Alfalfa Hay"
until Mom halted us. Daddy drove us
into the wheat field overgrowing the trail.

The car smelled like burnt toast from wheat and
grasshoppers clogging the Lincoln's engine.
Mom reminded my love he must marry me before
he would be permitted burial at the family cemetery.

My brother volunteered to be cemetery president,
if they wouldn't fight. He soon resigned.
The agenda includes: How do we encourage
the younger generation to participate?

Will the Rapid City bank pay better CD interest?
Why do we need approval for planting a shade tree?
Who will keep the cemetery records?
Why was a non-family neighbor buried there?

Uncle's wife asked why the gravel wasn't yet hauled
from Wall for fill-in at the gate. His donation
hit the treasury forty years ago. He's buried and
we still drive through muddy ruts.

Our family's genealogist wants to move
our oldest ancestors from Oelrichs
to welcome them to this family ground. Perhaps,
we should let my great-great-grandparents rest in peace.

The outhouse/shed was propped up
but totally blew apart in the last bad storm.
That concern will be added to our agenda.
Now, I wonder, where will we "go"?

For many absent times, distant residency
served as my viable excuse to avoid this obligation.
Mom skillfully played the guilt card and
reminded me the state requires an annual meeting.

She worried about Pierre* digging up Daddy.
I grumbled, "Okay. I'll be there this year.
What should I bring for the pot luck?"
Please, pray I keep my mouth shut.

*South Dakota State Capitol – pronounced *peer*

Original version written in 2005

Farewell to Pollen

Fare thee well pollen.
Be gone sneezing,
scratchy throat,
itchy eyes.

Rains, wash away
yellow powder
clinging to cars,
not pollinating any

flowers except this
dusty old rose who
loves spring but
hates pollen's sting.

Posted on Poetic Asides *2009*

Fat Chick

She's really hip,
and tummy,
and thighs,
but terribly wise.

Written in 2009

Fat Epitaph

This wife and mother lies, you know,
Where she can fit in her own row.
Not so tall, five-foot standing up.
Much wider than that she was, Yup.
Not very deep, but plenty wide.
There is no room on either side.

Written in 1983

Fences

High white stucco walls don't allow
passersby to see into the yard.
Lilac bush fences leave air heavy
with perfume. Decorative fences
don't keep anyone out or in.

Invisible fences intrigue me the most.
Manicured lawn ending on an invisible
straight line alongside that of one thick
with dandelions, white with seeded flowers.

Some invisible barriers keep people
away from loving other people.
We all erect fences from time to time.

Written in 1985

Fifth Anniversary

Cinnamon and I talked about you today.
We decided you definitely are a *keeper*.
We hope you'll continue to keep us too.

Sometimes on Saturdays we separate,
me to poetry class, you to the golf links,
each mining their own precious gold.

Back together we feel refreshed
and share in the other's treasures.
We fit, we belong, we're happy. Let's celebrate!

These five years have gone fast. We've had fun.
There are trillions more good memories than bad.
Here's to many more feelings of belonging with you.

I love loving you.

Written July 13, 2004

Finding Mary Again

Second grade, new school,
wrong house. I cried, "I'm lost."
Mary took my hand.

She walked me home.
She remembered
I was her new neighbor.

Her grades were all A's.
Mary knew our class's most elite.
She married a doctor.

Fifty years later, I bought her lunch,
asked if she wanted to visit
our old neighborhood.

"Oh, where would that be?" I drove us
to her childhood home. She pointed
across the street. "You lived there."

I was not sure until just then
that she remembered me. I'm so glad
we live somewhere inside her.

Mary can't remember what
word to call her husband,
or her sons' names and addresses.

I want to take her hand
and walk her memory through then
and back home to now.

Written in 2011

First I Lived

First I lived
and then I wrote
about my life.

Written in 2008

First Timers

Not perfect, but they were my parents.
It was all on-the-job training.
No practice sessions to be of the world.
Protect and isolate the family first.

They taught me many things
about humor in fun and cruelty,
about selective honesty. Okay to lie
but trained when only truth will do.

Serving others while slighting us.
Everyone else loved them as teachers.
Phase One of my character building,
and I'm quite a character.

Written in 2009

Flag

an Acrostic form

<u>F</u>reedom from tyranny,
<u>L</u>oyalty to the nation,
<u>A</u>gony in war,
<u>G</u>od's people prevail.

Written in September 2002

Flag Constellation

Tennessee's red, white and blue
mimics our national flag.
Like a constellation twinkles
on a clear night, she shines
her white stars in a primary blue ball.

Three five-pointed stars are grand divisions –
East, Middle, and West,
Clingman's Dome, Cumberland Plateau,
and Mississippi River,
Native American, African, and Caucasian,
Re-enactor, statesman, and patriot,
farmer, songster, and chemist,
mockingbird, ladybug, and firefly,
mussel pearl, Tulip Poplar, and iris,
My Tennessee, Rocky Top,
and The Tennessee Waltz,
soybean, cotton, and tobacco,
dairy, hogs, and cattle,
Volunteers, Butternuts, and Mid-South.

An unbroken band of pure white circles
unite to bind diversity together.
A stark crimson field contrasts blue and white
to wave bold and free in a once frontier land
tamed by humanity. A blue strip relieves
the eye from blood red when the flag is calm.
A perfect constellation for every state citizen.

Written in 2010

Flag Folding

I know why
Dad folded the flag
with my girl scout troop.
He insisted two young ladies
stand flag-length apart,
and not giggle.

They were to bring right hand
to left and match the edges.
Fold again into a long strip.
Red-striped side
walked the triangle folds
over and over
covering the blood red
with the blue valor
until the last corner
tucked into the edge.

No blood dripped
from our troop's resting flag.
No thread touched the floor.

Taps meant more to him
than Sunday best.
He honored numerous
veterans at funerals.
We moved Daddy's flag
to our family cemetery
where it flies over his grave.

2010 Written at Jane Hicks workshop sponsored by PST-NE

Flea Market Possession

Prisms play with light,
skip on the table,
glimmer with delight.

Facets, flaming stones,
once encircled neck,
impressed senile bones.

My fingers fiddle
with lingering life,
a sorrowful riddle.

Pressing through the past,
a glaring, scowling,
staring soul. I gasp.

Remembered warning:
used jewelry remains
a strayed soul's plaything,

sustains her story.
Glistening, it glows,
a cherished memory,

my thought erasure.
Fragments flash and wink.
I drop her treasure.

Prisms play with light,
skip on the table,
glimmer with delight.

*2005 Written in Rose Solari's Poem-A-Day class
at the Writers' Center,*
2007 published in Lost State Voices, *Volume II*

Flighty Business

Jonesy flew across the country often.
Perhaps because he dared not go home.
He denied having illicit affairs with women
half his own much advanced age.
Traveling from Los Angeles, he slept sound
on the overnight flight to New York.
Returned west he slumbered to Phoenix,
snored over Austin on up to Denver.
His pillow saw more miles than a pilot
who watched the patchwork
of plowed fields below.

Without family nor home place,
he solitarily ground out his business.
His loneliness drowned in first class seats.
He drained several glasses of champagne,
toasted each stewardess as she passed by.
Most giggled to his face, laughed behind him,
served dutifully to the rich passengers.
Growing more inebriated, he made
loving promises he was unable
to complete with any satisfaction.

His flight patterns became more erratic.
Poor business was nobody's business.
He claimed contentment flying annually,
but landed no new clients to advance his position.
Evidence of his extravagance trapped him
on his overdrawn expense accounts.
Energy saving accountants grounded
his flying style, claiming fuel saving miles.
Then business conference calls must suffice.
Instead of burning jet fuel, phone bills dialed.

One lovely lady missed him on her flights.
She kept his business card handy and called.
His line often busy, and her flight plans
filled, she saddened over his empty seat.
Passengers complained about sour-faced service.
Laid off with no pension, her career ended.
She tried his number one last time
before her bridge jump ended in cold water.
His number was redialed by police, but
he could not clearly recognize her name.

Written in 2009

Flora Sapiens

similar petals
in variant races

obsidian-diamond life:
  presses
  thinks
  plans

crème-opal being:
  absorbs
  caresses
  fascinates

achromatic-pearl entity:
  reflects
  illuminates
  shines

garnet-brick individual:
  clarifies
  builds
  paints

amber-chrome body:
  buffs
  squeezes
  sifts

sister flowers
many hues

all ask for:
  sun love
  earth nourishment
  rain respect

knowing the world holds
differences for each

Written in 2004

Flowers

I want to be like flowers.
Then, I wouldn't think or judge.
I'd look pretty and smell sweet.

Roots, leaves and thorns.
We're nothing grand
until we bloom.

I wish I were truly
a graceful flower,
not just a name.

Written in 2004

Foiled Again

a Dorsimbra form

This gravy appetite foils inner strength.
My greasy mind re-squeals for tasty breaks.
I think but naught – endure today full length.
These cravings end in snacks and milky shakes,

French fries, Swiss chocolate,
Italian bread, Hungarian Goulash.
Everything ethnic, anything
palatable, is acceptable.

My current biscuit powers weakest will
to motor mushy brain through rampant bites.
My inspiration nets more calories.
This gravy appetite foils inner strength.

Original written in 2009

Ford

Ford
azure, sapphire
driving, riding, hauling
truck, pick-up, vehicle, transportation
useful, helpful
Friend

1977 Written for DWU Creative Writing class

Four Corners

One huge foot stood in New Mexico,
a cramped toe tapped Arizona,
jumped into Utah and
crossed to Colorado.

No desert sands
differentiated the states.
They measured a crossroads
and marred it with concrete.

I walked back and forth
between joined states,
the Grand Canyon held less
fascination for a bored teenager.

For the family picture,
my tired bottom rested in
all four states at the same time.

Written in 2010

Free Dance

Isadora Duncan: May 26, 1877 – September 14, 1927
Creator of Modern Dance

Isadora Duncan
wrapped flowing scarves
about her dancing body.
Her world flashed
as flimsy as filmy fabric.

Scoffing at conventions
in ballet, she invented
modern dance, celebrated
natural curves and contours,
barely covered herself
with beloved scarves.

Defying all morals,
she danced to her own tune
with multiple lovers.
Life billowed like scarves
in the wind of motion.
Her last French words translated,
"Goodbye, my friend. I'm off to love."

She wrapped the streaming scarf,
dramatically about her neck,
not knowing it would betray her,
and become entangled in the spokes
of her lover's convertible wheels.

Constricting her neck,
that royal cloth invited her
to float free, dancing at last
fully unencumbered.

2010 2nd Place in PST 53rd Annual Mid-South Poetry Festival,
3rd Place Award 2011 and published in Echoes and Images

Freedom Fenced

I saw Freedom* fenced in today.
She stood straight and tall,
faced east, but with
scaffolds all around.

I thought about my freedom.
Terrorists tried to take that away.
Everyone is suspicious
since 9/11 infamy.

I am more cautious now.
I still think freely and
continue all I did before.
Fear fences me in less each day.

I'll never be a female warrior
in battle gear, but I will not
take freedom for granted nor
easily give it away.

*Freedom is the name of the female warrior statue
on top the Capitol building in Washington, DC

Written in 2002

Freely Breathe

I forget about breathing.
Breathing isn't a recreation.
Purely natural, breath is life.

I don't plan to breathe
next week or three times this week.
Breathing is not an exercise.

I just breathe. I don't
count it in and then count it out,
or write down today's progress.

If I thought about breathing,
I would pay attention to the air.
Maybe I should

demand air be toxin-free.
We could all benefit,
if we thought about breathing more.

Written in 2010

Friendship

People wonder
why we are friends.

We have different interests
and diverse beliefs.

But, we understand each other
and accept each other's viewpoints.

In that sense, we're the same.
Thus we'll remain friends.

Written in 1972

From Father to Grandfather

Where I didn't have a dime,
grandson is rich all the time.

They thought I was bad all along,
but it seems he can do no wrong.

The saying in Dad's day
(used almost every way),

Was *spare the rod and spoil the child*,
but grandchild's allowed to run wild.

Father used to spank, scold, and throw a fit,
but grandfather won't do that. Now I'm it.

When I grew up, it was going to be different.
Suddenly, I am the *heavy* the *establishment*.

Yes, for your information,
there's a strange transformation,

from when fathers are fathers,
until they are grandfathers.

Written in 1971

From Whence a Poem Comes

The beginning is a block of wood.
I imagine a coyote or winking duck.
I carve a few splinters, dig deeper,
and sand until smooth. I pet my creation
but get pricked by a missed sliver.
My little finger hurts and I suck
where the wood prods me.
Not quite finished, so I sand more
and cover with shellac until it gleams.
Then I might be happy with my poem.

2010 Written in Creative Writing Class at NeSCC

Frustrated Sky

The frustrated sky vanished in a blinding light.
Pellets of ice battered his windshield.
Spider webs formed across the glass.
Thunder grumbled. Clouds grew grimmer.
Sweat clung in bubbles, trickled down his profile.
More sauna steam was unwelcome inside his exit vehicle.
He wished she would rain cooler emotions.

Published on FanStory.com *in 2008*

Frustration

FRUSTRATION is:
    biting into a well-deserved hamburger
    while wide TV eyes stare from Third World hunger.

FRUSTRATION is:
    having a dollar bill when the change machine
    is out of order and no attendant on duty.

FRUSTRATION is:
    whispering words of love that are
    drowned out by your shouts of anger.

1977 Written for DWU Creative Writing class

Fun Food Thought

For a lifetime of enjoyment,
I suggest eating your way
through to the end.

Mom said, *Try everything*
three times before you
determine if you like it.

First time:
It may not be fixed properly.
Second time,
because it requires
an acquired taste.
If after the third time,
you pucker your lips
and shake your head,
definitely you don't like it.

I'm not yet sure I like pizza.
There are so many kinds:
thin crust, thick crust,
meat lovers, vegetable lovers,
with anchovies or without,
Sicilian, Italian, Chicago style.
I must try any and all combinations
at least three times before I decide.

If I don't keep good records,
I may have to start all over again.

Written November 2012

Funeral Procession

The television recorded Ronald Reagan's procession. Today, I won't sob so hard that I can't breathe, and then get so dry I can only squeeze out a tear or two to trickle down my cheek. Today, there are long lines of people waiting hour upon hour to pay respects. My thoughts turn to the thousands of minutes before my own son's death.

Ronald Reagan's body was flown in Air Force One to lie in state. In my son's hospital room, I swore his rhythmic breathing pushed the covers. Erik was transported as freight from the children's hospital to the funeral home. We were not allowed to carry him ourselves across state lines from Denver. It was a lonely six-hundred-mile drive home without his infectious smile.

I wondered what keepsake Nancy placed inside the president's casket. I remember the Christmas present, his father bought for our little boy. The fuzzy yellow bear bore Erik's nickname Tubby sewn on its name tag. My aching arms hugged bear's striped green T-shirt, kissed my older son's head. I stared at telephone poles dancing past us, when I silently reviewed his past days.

The former president's funeral broadcasted sad faces, recalled accomplishments. Erik lies in a child's grave marked, "Jesus Loves Me" and "Amen," those bedtime songs he'd squealed over and over again to accompany me. Unruly blond hair, somersaults, and bouncing dance amuse the angels in heaven. I hope they taught him to carry a tune and listen to the words.

Ronald Reagan was bigger than life. He did many things in his 93 years. My son is still aged two-and-a-half no matter how much time passes. It's been thirty years, but I remember his giggle and his fearlessness. Erik didn't have a riderless horse, a parade of people, or a sunset internment to symbolize his passing. In his short life, he touched a few people briefly.

Written in 2004

Garden of Eden

I wasn't there.
So, I'm not sure
what to believe.

If,
like gardens here,
I'd want to tour
and never leave.

2008 published in Barn Charm *chapbook*
and 2010 in the Appalachian Village Tower Chimes *newsletter*

Gardening Lessons

The first year in our house,
we planted a real yard.
We bought almost every plant
displayed at Wal-Mart and Lowe's.

We dug, fertilized mulched,
and anticipated a beautiful spring.
We smiled broadly
and patted our backs.

Then, drought slowed us down.
We didn't much like watering.
Our whole back hedge died off
with the crepe myrtle and dogwood.

We'd saved receipts, returned dead plants.
They refunded guaranteed ones.
It wasn't much solace for killing
off nature. We blamed lack of rain.

The drought challenged our hearty
Althea bush, two years running.
Or she didn't much like
the hard-packed red clay.

The lawnmower ran over
her remains. We'd given up
planting new until the rains
would catch up the water table.

We thank God for moisture.
Amazing, Althea, aka *Rose of Sharon*,
peeks out of the gravel
and drinks the run off.

Aw, spring has sprung
and so have sprouts.
Maybe our brown thumbs
have turned. Green is reborn.

Posted on Poetic Asides *2009*

Garden Path Jog

My heartbeat rhythm runs fast
like a panting gazelle fleeing
the stalking lioness's lunch plans.
All around our favorite walking park,
my husband spirals me.
His heart doesn't lurch
but is slow as a slug
sneaking through the grass
to ruin our tomatoes.
He speeds me up.
I slow him down.

*2008 Written in Anne Barnhill's class to the prompt – gazelle/lunch
at the South Carolina Writers Workshop (SCWW), Myrtle Beach, South
Carolina*

Gertrude Grace (Olmstead) Rose

*Dedicated to my Dakota Territory pioneer grandmother:
2 April 1886-21 October 1967*

I'd volunteered to accompany Mother
when she nursed Fred's sister-in-law.
I fell in love. Before marriage,
we each staked a claim and built
our prairie dug-out home.
Fred's pet bull snake kept rattlers
out of our soddy. He was a jack-of-all-trades
and kept things and the family together.
We laid our newborn twins in the Rose Family Cemetery.
Losing babies was hard, but we conceived more.

I was a young pregnant widow,
when I buried my Fred.
I owned two homestead sections, but
had no real home. I gave up and walked
my children a hundred miles to family help.
We survived the best we could.
Seven called me mother.

I buried Joe, my second husband,
and raised our daughter.
Too many called me Grandma.
Nieces called me Aunt Gertie,
but I preferred the gentler Grace.

One biting cold October I returned
to this prairie. Wind pressed without resistance.
I wasn't warm here for eighty-one years and
haven't been warm since. I find no comfort
in granite and sagebrush and would welcome
one of Mother's woven rugs or my own quilts.

Perhaps I should settle
for just a pleasant thought
or enduring memory.

Written in 2009

Rose Klix

GI Party

Ah, Gee,
is it that time again already?

Gee, I thought
it was just a year ago.

GI Parties
are prevalent

to prepare for the
IG.

Written in 1990

Giant Mistakes

At six-foot-twelve Dan leaned
ape-like arms on the gallows bracket.
Strips of fringe dangled from
his favorite buckskin jacket.

He wouldn't even hurt a gnat.
At his trial no one believed,
he didn't harm the little girl.
Actually, the town was relieved.

The court sentence would rid them
of the freak they despised and their
guilt in not finding Lizzy girl.
Few showed any amount of care.

He shrugged off his mom's clinging hug.
She looked up at her baby.
Dan demanded, "Don't cry in public."
Then nudged her to go away.

A blackened toothy grin sickened
the crowd, who booed and hissed him.
Rotten fruit smacked on his jacket.
He kicked some muck back at them.

He roared, but couldn't brush away
the mess with hands tied in back.
The hangman forced him to kneel and
over his head secured a black sack.

The rope held, but the wood frame broke.
The hangman could hear Dan's hoarse
whisper, "She's gone to her home now."
Appeased, people exited the concourse.

The sheriff, coroner, and about
seven men total, removed the bum.
Lizzy's dad appeared and cried,
"She's okay. My girl came home!"

Written in 2009

Gift of the Eagle's Feather

In memory of my brother James Orion Rose:
May 28, 1948 - May 24, 2009

Traveling I-90 West I packed my brother's remains
home to the Black Hills.
His simple urn was filled heart-heavy with wishes
of unfulfilled purposes.

He'd become Indian in his forties. I found
no genealogy to prove him right.
Still his smoke-wrinkled, toothless face smiled.
His gray hair grew long braids.

He drummed in tribal circles and displayed
a turquoise amulet on his chambray
western shirt snapped with pearl fasteners,
insistent, he was Indian from any tribe.

I pulled to the highway's shoulder and stopped.
Childhood memories filled my eyes.
I imagined hearing a mournful chant
around a pine-log scented fire.

The eagle feather drifted, settled directly
on my windshield.
I stopped myself short from turning on the wipers,
to sweep it away into the night.

I looked over my shoulder, plucked it
quickly from the wiper blade,
and laughed at my strict caution.
No chance anyone saw in the dark.

I knew only verified Indians are allowed
possession of an eagle's feather.
I fanned the shaft, all perfectly intact.
In my dome light its purity glistened.

Absolute white contrasted a black tipping.
I thought of a writer's quill, then quickly
dismissed the idea of mundane labor.
Improbability wondered at an eagle

losing this one feather to land on my car
at that exact moment. I shivered,
snapped the locks, but spirits stayed.
I placed it on the small square box.

The closer I came to the Black Hills the more
naturally the feather rested on the urn.
This was a gift, not to me, but to my brother
for honoring his imaginary ancestry.

You won't tell. I buried the eagle's feather too.
It was a gift, not to a Native American,
but to an American native who honored traditions
I can only wish I understood.

2008 1ˢᵗ Place in PST Mid-South Festival and
published in Tennessee Voices *2008-09*

Go Ahead

Go ahead:
  tell me I am nothing,
  tell me I'm lost,
  tell me I'm ugly,
  and love-crossed.

I'm not famous.
  I'm not rich.
  I'm not beautiful,
  and boy I could bitch.

I have complaints,
  mostly of you
  telling me what I'm not.
  But I'll not boo hoo.

I'll hide my ugly side,
  and toughen my goals,
  reach for the heavens
  and join the choir of lost souls.

Written in 2010

Go Around

Trail around the trees,
without severe straight lines.
Merciful engineers, please
plan without eliminating
gradual growing trees.
Remove trash not timber.
Reforestation is interminable.

2005 published in Schrom Hills Park *chapbook*

Go Away, Angels

Hope is in your hands.
Grasp the air around me.
Do not breathe your anxiety
or exhale despair at me.
Watch only if you can
brighten these minutes.

Sift your thoughts,
comb out dark grains,
enhance mica sparkles,
and smile – and smile.
I want to hold smiles.

Go away, angels.
I am not done yet.
The family's after-death
poker game will play without me.
I refuse to accept my epitaph today.

Written in 2010

Go on Now

You taught me, *Grab all the gusto!*
I learned craft on my own.
You noticed my rejections.

My career soared and skydived.
Your hand reached my pocket,
but didn't break my fall.

I sang sweetly for others
at public recitals, you missed –
otherwise occupied.

You were too busy
grabbing the gusto
with a twenty-one year old.

I succeeded without you.
Don't ride my coattails.
The parade passed. *Go on now.*

1977 Written for DWU Creative Writing class

God and Country

God bless our country.
Guide our decisions for war.
Grant us peace and love.
Help us to live as before.

Written in 2002

God, How Much is Enough?

How much life do I need
to experience, before
I can enjoy it?

How much money do I need
to save? How much time
do I have to waste?

When, God, when?
When may I retire
from this life's work?

Written in 2004

God, My Greatest Love

Loving more than anyone else can,
God is my greatest love.
His love surrounds me.
In my imperfection,
He loves me anyway.

The beginning and the end,
without Him there is no one else.
His love multiplies to reach infinity.
He loves me when I'm not loveable.
Patiently, He helps me to improve.

He gave his Son, Jesus, to die for me.
Because I am human and frail,
He sends his Holy Spirit to me.
Knowing I need all the help He can give,
He encourages with faith, hope, and love.

The greatest of these is my love from the
Father, Son, and Holy Ghost. Amen.

Published 1999 in The Messenger, *2005 in* Faith and Spirit *chapbook, and 2010 in* Spiritual Reflections *PST-NE's Anthology*

God's Paintbrushes

Each blessed day God paints us a masterpiece.
The sky clears His perfect canvas.
He brushes clouds into rearrangements
with strong winds or gentle breezes
across His chosen blue pallet.
Occasionally, He paints white gesso horizons;
then we must wait for future decorations.

Written in 1978

Golden Ekphrastic

In honor of: Van Gogh's painting titled Wheat Field with Crows

A smudge of sunlight lost
the day's gold medal
to wind-fanned wheat shafts.
The sky caldron swished to spill crows
gleaning the field brown.
Our muddy road swiveled her hips
seeking a silver moon all the way home.

*2010 Written during a class taught by Poet Laureate of Virginia
Carolyn Kreiter-Foronda.,
2011 3rd Place in the Blue Plum Festival's poetry contest
sponsored by Johnson City Public Library, Tennessee*

Golden Sky

Golden sky behind
bare branches –
brisk walk.

Written in 2005

Goofing Off

He could sniff out golf courses
faster than Canada geese
located a puddle of water.
One day, he yellow-sprayed
the wood hazard.
Air Force One flew by,
returning the President
from a local town meeting.
Big Brothers watched.
Satellite images didn't show
the man's exposed putter.
The Secret Servicemen laughed,
wanted to join him for a golf game,
wished for their turn to goof off.

Written in 2009

Grabawil

(from Under the Frozen Lake)

a Jabberwocky parody

'Twas benchald, and the cresly jodes
did wimple and yankle in the glabe:
All prassy were the amnagodes,
and the frome dades pansrabe.

Beware the Grabawil, my child!
The looks that sear, the ice that cracks!
Beware the Dindin fish, and the defiled
the sniprous Justerbacks!

She grabbed my dankal piece from me.
Long time all pendazzle friends she left –
so rested she by the Limpramble tree,
and leaned awhile by the cleft.

And, as in irumpish thought she'd sink.
The Grabawill, with gills of pain,
came vampling through the wastul rink,
and cried as it became!

Ten, twelve! Twelve, ten! It bled and screeched.
The dankal piece went janker-jack!
She left it dead, and with it beached
she went benjarring back.

And, has thou slain the Grabawill?
Come to dinner, my simple one!
O weemerose day! Janjeep! Jallay!
She panriled about what was won.

'Twas benchald, and the cresly jodes
Did wimple and yankle in the glabe:
All prassy were the amnagodes,
and the frome dades panrabe.

2010 3rd Place in PST Annual Mid-South Poetry Festival and
2011 Published in PST-NE's Humorous Collection Funny you should say that. . .

Grandfather Barn

Woods and wood
trees and barn,
weathered and worn,
remind us of tobacco fields
and country roads.
Hold off steel and concrete.
Gray and brown,
stand your ground.

2008 published in Barn Charm *chapbook*

Grandpa Swinehart

Dedicated to my grandfather Orion Wyant Swinehart:
28 May 1896 – 19 November 1983

Through his jokes,
he taught me humor
and swear words.

Severely colorblind,
he practiced drawing
with pen and ink.

As he aged,
he reflected and
taught me of his youth.

He heard less,
spoke quieter
and much slower.

He left me tales
of the Old West
to remember him.

Written in 1987

Grassroots

a Korean Sijo form

Rain pounded my pink petunias, wiggled rooted toes in mud pies.
Clever clover blossoms popped up, dotted ankle-high grass.
Rain teamed sun to grow wild onions, our lawnmower soon tamed.

2009 3rd Place September PST monthly contest
and 2010 published in Lost State Voices, Volume III

Gratuity

You plop change
in my outstretched
palm not counting
it back proper.
You're baffled,
when the register
loses electricity.

Slow service,
botched order,
meat arrived cold,
catsup stuck.
Requested straw
didn't materialize
nor a water refill.

You tap your fingers
on the table and
shrug to the next
impatient customer.
I file the receipt,
fold the bills, and
pocket the coins.

For your tip,
I say thank you,
because I think
one of us is
required to do so.

Written in 2005

Graveyard Memorials

Your death has been perpetuated forever.
There is only a pile of unattended memories.
Once you must have been loved for ages.
Now the life and spirit is gone.

Love carved your stone with facts.
Now sentiments are barely legible.
Dust we are and to dust we all return.
Still we leave behind meaningless granite.

Written in 2004

Gravitational Pull

This year our constellation
skewed further and further
Northeast beyond Orion's belt
where a cluster of planets and asteroids
circle your star, reflect your presence,
and sunbathe in your spotlight.
I hover on the horizon and gasp.
Should I twinkle in your direction
or join the orbit around a dimmer sun?

2010 1ˢᵗ Place, February PST monthly contest
and published in Tennessee Voices Anthology 2009-2010

Great Creator

Thank you, God, for creating
the Word: the beginning
of expression for me and through me.
Your light shines within each person.
I look to you for inspiration,
full of gratitude for my talents and gifts.
My imaginary worlds are imperfect.
I ask for your assistance, because I am
a poor imitator of Your creative powers.
I ask Your blessings on my works,
and on all attempts to craft my creations
for universal understanding of Your Word.
Amen

2012 Written as an invocation and
published in Grandmother Earth Volume XIX

Grits is It's!

Breakfast? Yummy.
Wake up, tummy.
Look! Bits of grits.

Cornflakes fizzled.
Syrup drizzled,
can't disguise grits.

Poke each taste bud.
Chew like cow cud.
Always it's grits.

Try cheese melted.
Mad Paw unbelted.
I swallow down grits.

Written in 2009

Growing Up

Someday,
you're goin'
to be a man.
What you can't, now.
Then you can.

Written in 1985 for my then teenage son.

Gum on the Metro Posts

Don't lean on these posts,
because you don't know
just what may be on them.
At least I can see the gum.
The other microscopic yuk is
invisible to the naked eye,
but then so are the microbes,
in the very air we breathe.
Whatever you've breathed out,
I just breathed in.
Ooooh.

Written in 2004

Halloween Headstone

Genealogical research
is like digging up bones.
One day, I rubbed
a graphite pencil on legal size
paper held against a tombstone.

Incomplete dates and names
magically appear. I feel like
Aladdin rubbing his lamp.
Giggling, I wonder about a genie's
three wishes I'm to be granted.

I frown at crumbling stones
and am dismayed to see
an almost illegible legend.
Squint-eyed I stare against the sun's glare.
A figure startles me.

Mrs. So and So says,
What is my name? She cries.
I shrug and blink my widened eyes.
I do not know. It's not clear.
I read, *Mrs. Jo----n, bl---ed wife of C-ar-es,*
mother of Sa---h, 19y, -m, 1-d

*What was **my** name?* She implores.
***My** name? Didn't **I** have a name?*
*Wasn't **I** someone? Granny knows.*
Her blue gown trails her transparent body.
She searches for another tombstone.

Where is she? Where is Granny Brown?
Other figures rise in the crisp October air.
They ask, *What is this sad forgotten place?*
I'm not the caretaker of old cemeteries.
I cannot answer ancient questions for lost souls.

I thought Johnson may be the link.
I was thrilled I might find my answers.
My third great-grandmother died
before she was twenty.
Could you have been Mary, called Polly?

Polly? She turns in recognition
but rages at me. She shrieks.
I hate my brother's nickname.
Polly Wolly, tadpole, old toad. Is he here too?
Joshua, Josh. He was always teasing me.
Her face crowds my space.

I feel where her breath once was.
I query, What's his name?
I flipped my ancestral papers.
Was he Joshua Brown? She glares.

The Browns moved on to Ohio.
Josh followed the gold to California.
Never did hear from him again.
Probably he struck it rich and
didn't want to share – like usual.
I'm glad he didn't carve
Polly on my stone.

She looks over my shoulder.
I turn my recorded pages.
I read her history, our family connections.
Slowly, her finger traces her name.
Mary "Polly" Brown,
married Charles Johnson,
She cries. *Dear, dear, Charles.*

At that first harvest dance, he shuffled
his feet and cleared his throat before
asking to walk me home.
His eyes were so blue and that
bright red hair defied a comb.

He took a fever real bad
and died ten days after fragile Sarah.
I watched them bury both
before my twentieth birthday.

All alone in that sanitarium,
no one cared enough to remember my name.
I was forever just wife of Charles
and mother of little Sarah.
That's who I was and who I'll always be.

I try to speak. She begs me
turn more pages, show her my notes.
I read:. . .died giving life to Samuel.

Yes, I gave birth at St. Anne's Sanctuary.
My heart broke when they stole him from me.
I tell her family stories about Samuel,
and his half dozen children. We laugh.

The wind blows more golden leaves
from the trees. Jealous spirits watch us,
wish for descendants to celebrate
All Saints Day with them.
We part before dark. I promise
to return another day.

Published on FanStory.com *2008*

Pastiche of Poetry

Hammers

a Quinzaine form

Hammers pounding in rhythm.
Ambitious builders
make my dream?

1977 Written for DWU Creative Writing class

Happy First Anniversary

It has been a full year,
full of flowers and loving consideration,
full of growth and love,
and learning about each other.

We've seen the best of places
and interesting times.
We've helped each other through a few
rough times and bad health.

I've felt loved and protected,
become part of you, and
you've become part of me.
But yet, I'm allowed to be myself.

Thank you for this the best year
of our married life so far.

Written January 13, 1992

Happy Now?

I hope you laugh now, Mom.
I won't ever again nag you to eat
something good for you
prescribed by assisted living.
Enjoy your mashed potatoes,
cookies, and ice cream.

You disappointed me, because you couldn't enjoy
theatre outings and country drives together.
I dictated to you frequently
as you became less my mom
and more a responsibility.

I hated mediating with center staff.
You hated bingo and the forced Sunday social time.
You complained about living in a prison.
They said, "You can't bloom in your room."
You replied, "I'll bloom anywhere I want."

You lived eighty-five years
choosing your own life path.
You said you'd accomplished everything
you wanted and didn't regret anything.
Now, I know you're floating freely,
dancing the foxtrot and jitterbug with Dad.

Posted on Poetic Asides *2009*

Harvesting Smiles

You beam
like you won
the Power Ball.
Eyes gleam
with delight.

Your pride
seared
like sunshine
melting snow.
What is it?

I relished your mood.
"Look." You offer
your outstretched
Wal-Mart plastic bag.
I see dirt-crusted cucumbers,

vine-ripened tomatoes,
green peppers, zucchini,
and yellow squash –
your garden harvest,
an all organic inventory.

2008 published on All Things Girl.net *an e-zine*

Hatful

Hats aren't accepted
as fashionable.
I'm tired
of hats and wigs
itching my head
and people staring.

Only trusted family
and friends have seen
what isn't under my hat.
Soon I shall shed
my camouflage chapeaus
like a cocoon.
As soon as my hair
is filled in enough,
I'll style it.

Only my husband
knows the trauma
I experienced when
handfuls of hair sat
in the bottom
of the shower.
I'd been told
it would just thin.
Then, I waited years
to grow back thick.

Written in 2010 during Jane Hicks workshop sponsored by PST-NE.

Hawk's Trap

Frosted grass,
crisp air,
clear December day,
birdfeeder watching
during breakfast.

Hawk swoops down.
Blood spatters siding,
splashes window.
Dropped gray feathers float
onto dormant roses.

Quiet feeder for days:
cardinals, sparrows,
blue jays, and the woodpecker,
gone elsewhere for food.

Hawks must get hungry,
but surely dine on rodents.
We feel implicated
in mourning dove's murder.

Nevertheless, my husband
decides to refill the feeder.
I fear he probably
reloaded the hawk's trap.

Written in 2011

Heartless Wind

inspired by the prairie winds of Mitchell, South Dakota

an Adagem form

THE weather became
      cold and wet. Heartless
WIND blew. Prairie
      dissolved in mud. A chill
HAD hollowed the land. My infatuation
      disappeared. The wind had
BLOWN a chill in my heart. I once
      loved the warm gentle breezes as
MY comfortable friends patted my head and
      teased my hair. My cold
HEART hates the wind
      tearing at the land. Go
AWAY torrents of rain.
      Take the cruel wind with you.

*1977 Written for DWU Creative Writing class
and 1978 published in* CMA Review *anthology*

Heaven on Earth

Inspired by the Cathedral Spires, Needles Highway, Black Hills, South Dakota

My earthly heaven sits
above the hurry and noise.
Its arched gateway opens
for all to enter this paradise.
Fiercely sculpted by wind and rain,
jagged rocks pierce the sky.
Golden brown earth possesses
each scattered patch of green.
See the stately ponderosa pine trees.
Hear quiet whispers of winged voices.
Wind ruffles my hair
tickles the treetops.
Any minute a cloud
will dissolve into an angel,
who sits atop an unpolished pillar.
Survey my heaven.
Come, hike, and laugh with me.
Play tag through the *Needle's Eye*,
then show me your heaven on earth.

Originally written in 1969. 2003 published in The Way of the Cross *and in PST-NE's 2011* Images of Love *Anthology*

Heavenly Garden of Eden

I want dearly to believe.
Paradise, ah, but where?
Heaven thoughts make me grieve.

Sometimes, I want my home there.

Perhaps, I would not want to leave,
if perfection were here.
Then angels might be relieved.

Written in 2010

Hello, Patriotism, Where Have You Been?

I used to see your flags and colors
paraded on the streets of my hometown.
Obvious signs of you were long absent.

You were virtually invisible until lately.
Have you been hiding in VFW halls?
Or in pages of my history books?

What a shame it takes a nine-eleven tragedy
to awaken our national awareness.
Hello, Patriotism – Welcome back!

Written in 2003,
2010 Honorable Mention in the Blue Plum Poetry Festival
sponsored by the Johnson City Public Library, Tennessee

Here and Gone

Here in April.
Gone in June.
The barn's rubble
stacked too soon.

2008 published in Barn Charm *chapbook*

Heroes and Heroines

Fire fighters,
police officers,
do their duty
as heroes and heroines.

We call upon
our guardsmen
to protect,
fill military void.

Heroes, heroines
like normal people
are really the same.
Label depends
on situation.

Written in 2002

Hole in My Heart

Isn't it funny?
A hole in my ear doesn't hurt
though I stab it every day
with a jeweled stud.
But a prick in my heart
hurts for my whole life.

Written in 2004

Home

Floor, ceiling, walls
I couldn't ask for more.
That's what makes up a home.

Kitchen, living room, bedroom
That's about all I need.
What's missing? Why isn't it a home?

Furniture, bath, windows
I have everything I want.
Why doesn't it feel like a home?

You walked in the door, and
I knew our home was just right.

Written in 2004

Homecoming

Mom's middle name was
Impatience. She just wanted to
get on with it, and said,

The horses are getting
restless. They'd been
bridled a very long time.

In her morphine trance,
she saw people lined up
on both sides of the street.

A glorious parade waited
for her homecoming.
Does this seem real to you?

No, Momma, it doesn't.
I squeezed her hand,
assured her Daddy was waiting.

A tear dribbled towards her ear.
We both giggled and remembered
one of Dad's favorite sayings.

I have tears in my ears
from lying on my back
crying over you.

Her last hours weren't what I expected.
Her homecoming parade reassured me
she wouldn't be alone.

Posted on Poetic Asides *2009*

Honeysuckle Moose

Voila! Imagine
a honeysuckle moose
in our park.
We paused, stared
at a surprising reminder of
our Alaskan tour
here in natural topiary.
We pulled nectar from blossoms,
drank to our health,
and thanked him for standing
proud guardian of our forest.

2005 published in Schrom Hills Park *chapbook*

Honoring Mom

Three newspapers published
your picture and obituary.

Besides me and my husband,
three people showed up.

One lady had never met you.
She came because of my book club.

You were virtually unknown
to the pastor conducting the service.

He kept calling me by the name
you gave me at birth, the one I hate,

the name you listed in your autobiography.
You'd always insisted calling me that anyway.

I dread going through this again
in your home town next month.

I hope they remember you, but will they
realize I'm not who you wanted me to be?

Posted on Poetic Asides *2009*

Hooked on Books

Friends be forewarned:
clever lures appear on book jackets.
For many years, tasty hooks
have fed this avid reader.

Clever plots and strange
characters turn night to dawn.
I swallow the fiction bait,
and want freedom from my reality.

Novel bribery catches
me deep in every library.
I swim past schools of thought
until I'm reeled in, then pant for air.

The stacks seem to troll by me.
I'm caught holding a boatload of books.
They will release me until next week,
when I know nets will be cast again.

Written in 2010 in Creative Writing class at NeSCC,
2010 won 3rd Place in PST Annual Mid-South Festival and
2011 published in Echoes and Images

Hope Revealed

Angry stubborn stubbles
reached through the snow.
Harsh fields revealed hope.

Lost kernels mocked the reaper.
A tractor whispered idleness.
In the spring, he nodded.

His promise threatened
tracks of dark earth.
Work will cover their smirks.

His shadow hovered over them,
vowed to plow fertile ground,
and start again fresh next spring.

1977 Written for DWU Creative Writing class

Horns

Horns
harassing, friendly
honking, blasting, tooting
anger, communication, danger, greeting
helpful, disturbing
signals.

1977 Written for DWU Creative Writing class

Hot Air Balloon Ride

Bright primary colors stripe the balloon, contrast blue sky.
Above the flame, I see a peaceful abstract picture.
The air is almost still – just enough breeze to push us along.

Neighborhood dogs greet us, sound the alarm, and run away.
Area residents point at us. We wave, but
turn down a coffee invitation. We prefer to float.

The pilot says he must ascend again.
We applaud, but hold our breath until we've topped the trees.
I watch our shadow decrease on the ground.

We welcome quiet when the pilot turns off helium flames,
and the balloon lands gently in an open field. This brings us back
to earth and reality. Neighbors mob us for short rides,
while my husband helps hold the tethers.

Often I close my eyes when I want to float, not think about daily chores.
I imagine I'm again nine-hundred feet above the ground.

I want to sing like a sparrow after a stormy day. The ride was over too soon.
When I'm typing, the phone is ringing, and I'm late, I'll remember this day.
Thank you, God, for the opportunity to float above my troubles.

2005 published in Faith and Spirit *chapbook*

How Much Love?

If you ask me how much I love you,
I'd ponder how much I love life.
What would I give up to be with you?
My eyesight is precious to me.
I don't need to see the pink and gold
blended sunset, or a fawn hiding
behind his mother, but I do want to see
your wind-tossed hair and your blue eyes.

Written in 2004

Huge Hugs

Hugs are huge from laughing
outstretched brown arms
encircling a small shy niece.

Great-uncle Bill's husky laugh
rippled the gold-mined creek
in Mystic, South Dakota.

He pop-topped glass bottles
from his own country store
across the graveled road.

Great-aunt Irene picked wild
daises and made spicy
watermelon rind pickles.

Their outhouse was designated
an official historic landmark
preserving memories of good times.

They giggled and waited
as I experienced my first
trip to the two-holer.

Uncle Bill died, and then
I learned prejudice first hand.
Dad surprised me saying,

"Good thing they didn't have children."
I was doubly shocked, when I learned
my beloved great-uncle was black.

I learned Bill wasn't suntanned
from forest ranging. I said, "I don't care."
Everyone's color is only skin deep.

I loved him before and then
even more, because he hadn't
changed – just Dad and me.

Uncle Bill's eyes sparkled with mica.
His heart was amber as Black Hills gold.
I miss his laughing huge hugs.

Written in 2008,
2011 3rd Place in Poetry Society of Virginia contest

Huggy Thoughts

I'm so huggy now.
I hold on for fear of leaving
or fear of staying.
Not from practicing Southern living,
perhaps this fear stems from old age.
I want a hug.
I miss Dad, Mom, and Jim.

Written in 2009

Humans Get Cancer

I dragged myself into the cancer clinic.
Alternative treatments disappointed me,
and did not slow my tumor's growth.

Rows upon rows of straight-backed chairs
lined the waiting room. We faced
the glassed-in reception desk,
as if they feared we were contagious,
dangerous, or wanted special attention.

After waiting an hour, I was called.
I hate my full name. Politely,
I requested the phlebotomist
call me Rose. She marked my chart
and introduced herself as Katie.

I sat in the lab for the extraction
of vial after vial of blood-letting –
seventeen tubes. I almost fainted.
My blood pressure registered very, very
high when compared to my normal.

I cried uncontrollably at surrendering
to the chemo-poison promised
to save my life. I already subjected my body
to double mastectomy surgery.
Mutilation and poison are medically best choices?

Katie treated me as other than a number
in the busy clinic. We hugged. She wiped my tears,
and promised to take care of me as if I were her grandma.
She always remembered to call me by my preferred name,
a feat no one else there could duplicate.

She smiled at me every week. Katie patted my hand
before taking my blood to a cloistered technician.
Only to her, was I human. I almost looked forward
to seeing Katie's curly red hair and friendly freckled face.
I miss her hugs, but vow to never go there again.

Written in 2011

Hummingbird Feeder

Four related Haiku form

A red feeder is
full of fresh wild songbird seeds.
Loud buzz hums hunger.

Hummingbird complains.
Welcome! Red Shirt speaks greeting.
Confusion hovers.

Shopping trip required
to buy sugar-water kit,
feed small family.

Feeder nourishes,
sweetens hummingbird's long flight,
our daily pleasure.

Written in 2010

Hunger Appeased

a Haiku form

Hunger swoops down from
the sky, catches a beetle,
glides away, appeased.

1989 published in Dakota: Plains & Fancy *for the Vermillion Literary Project,
South Dakota and 2010 in* Grandmother Earth, *Volume XVI*

Hungry Outside

It gets hungry outside,
when home is far away.
That is the kind of hunger
which gnaws at the heart.

It gets hungry outside when there's no home to go to.
It gets lonely outside when there's no one to talk to.
It gets cold outside when there's no one to hug.
It gets tired outside when there's no bed to snuggle in.

I experienced hunger
that pulls at the heart.
strong enough for me to admit
my mistake in thoughts of leaving him.

Written in 1985

J

I am But One

a Pantoum form

I realize, I am but one
among the total universe.
You think your earth revolves the sun.
What if one day the poles reverse?

Among the total universe,
so many worlds I hoped to see.
What if one day the poles reverse,
submerges land, lost at sea?

So many worlds I hoped to see.
Not all the countries I've explored,
when land submerged, lost at sea.
I do regret some space adored.

Not all the countries I've explored
have nooks where chemicals abound.
I do regret some space adored.
Will earth again be sacred ground?

Nooks stay where chemicals abound.
Your earth may still revolve the sun.
I do regret some space adored.
I realize, I am but one.

Written in 2011

I am From

I'm from Hangman's Hill and Black Hills,
     Rapid Creek duck races,
     ponderosa pine trees and blue spruce,
     backyard swing and munches on grass blade roots,
     Dinosaur Hill and Pioneer Museum, and
     Main Street window shopping on Sunday afternoons.
I'm from lemon meringue pie on Thanksgiving with the Roses
 and player piano Christmases with the Swineharts,
     dipping hot buttered toast in hot chocolate,
     Dad blowing smoke in my aching ear,
     Mom ignoring me in Girl Scout meetings, and
I'm from Snookie, my dog, licking my tears away.

Written in 2011

Icy

Icy
soothing, cooling
suppressing my hot thirst
Popsicle

1977 Written for DWU Creative Writing class

I Hate Carrots

a Concrete or Picture form

I despise
nauseous,
orange
mealy-
flavored,
narrow,
crooked
roots.
When
starving,
look for
what is
good.
Carrots?
Scrape,
scrape
off dirt.
Crunch.
Ugh!
No!

1977 Written for DWU Creative Writing class

I Just Need

I just need air,
Rob, and Cinnamon
first thing in the morning.
No caffeine or sugar
poison my day.
After my shower
wake up call, everything
fast-forwards to the office,
where I sip my first
tall glass of spring water.

Written in 2004

Indian Appellations

a Reflection form

Our
natives,
Columbus
named when too lost.
Glad he did not aim
for Turkey. Drumsticks
are tastier
than misplaced
ethnic
names.

2010 3rd Place PST Annual Mid-South Poetry Festival

Infamous Unknown

a La'Tuin form

I was plagued with immobility.
Patience was not in my bloodline.
No good mentors traveled upper-class.
Life didn't bring tranquility.

I sang each works' audibility.
Hymns and masters framed my baseline.
Formal forms, poets often bypass
for muse accountability.

Then questioning my ability,
success was foreign, borderline.
Within literal worlds I trespassed,
discovered flammability.

Thoughts and moments boast fragility.
My name disappeared from headline.
Time and money threshold at impasse.
Life ended in humility.

I was plagued with immobility.
Patience was not in my bloodline.
No good mentors traveled upper-class.
Life didn't bring tranquility.

Published on FanStory.com in 2009

In Mourning

The squirrel's palms pressed
against his plump chest.
His cloudy eyes
barely blinked. He was

not begging today
nor did he sprint
from my whispered,
"Are you all right?" He was

not caring the Capitol
passed the largest deficit
ceiling in history or they'd
voted *No* to my pay raise. He was

not concerned about
fire engines squealing
to a restaurant fire
by Union Station. He was

a rodent statue watching
into eternity as a dear
departed friend's
spirit disappeared. She was

lying nearby, her softness
became a stiff empty shell,
her last glimpse of sky forever
captured in her gaze.

He ignored his comrades
who beckoned him
to tree-chase up to her
woven nest.

He held his heart, momentarily,
watched something silently
slip into forgetfulness
of who they once were.

Written in 2004 in a Washington, DC park

Insect Philosophy

If it's not bugging you,
why do you bug it?
Don't poke at a hornet's nest
full of negative energies.

Whisper butterfly's fluttering.
Sing like dragonfly wings.
Drink rose perfume
and sup on fallen peaches.

Ride the wind.
Shower in the rain.
Rebuild knocked down webs.
Capture life in your net.

Written in 2004

Inspiration

Creation is power.
I ask that You, God, my greatest inspiration,
be present today and always.
Without You in my life I could not write.
Creative energies sparkle in the room.
I am abuzz, sometimes afraid, to express
my buried thoughts and emotions.
My ideas were not created in a void.
I write in accordance with: Your training,
my experiences, interactions and feelings.
Each spark first came from You.
Help illuminate my words.
Your inspiration empowers me.
I pray that all my words begin with goodness
and spread Your greatness,
reflect Your light.
Amen

Written in 2012 as an invocation

Inspired Magically

Inspiration is magical,
sparks action,
enflames ideas,
heats discussions,
smolders until rekindled.

Words fly into print,
carefully considered
before real work begins
through hours, days, weeks,
months, years, decades
of perspiration
until overnight
a poet is declared
successful.

Written in 2010

Interwoven Arts

Colorful
shapes, designs
fashion artistic pictures.

Words,
sentences, paragraphs
make thoughtful images.

Colorful
sentences, paragraphs
fashion artistic pictures.

Words,
shapes, designs
make thoughtful images.

Colorful
sentences, designs
make thoughtful pictures.

Words,
shapes, paragraphs
fashion artistic images.

1977 Written for DWU Creative Writing class

Iris Gift in Autumn

You are confused and I am confused by
your strange behavior. You didn't bloom the last
two springs and yet now I cry.
I see your golden blossom heaven cast.

When did you decide to try?
Was it last winter or in the middle
of this drought? Under October's bluest sky,
you now see me here asking my riddle.

The greenhouse said you are just now mature.
You could be the type to flower twice.
I hope you flourish here every year.
Either way, welcome. Nice surprise, before winter's ice.

Written in 2008

I Think I Look Like Lunch Today

I think I must look like lunch today.
I watch the tiger pace her cage.
She roars, grumbles, and kicks her pan.
Meal time was more inviting in the jungle.

Lunch must have been more appealing on the run.
She sees me, bares teeth, smacks her lips.
Her zoo lunch may be delivered now
or perhaps I'll say goodbye and back away.

Written in 2009

Jet Propelled DNA

a Minute form

Will science now affirm to us,
   (with fanfare fuss)
    a molecule
    to ridicule?
These cells unwind so small, and yet:
    my life's birth jet,
    a blueprint chock,
    no one should mock.
Existence tentative at best,
    not knowing quest,
    I seek my truth,
    not science booth.

Written in 2011

Just a Sliver of Stolen Crumbs

Momma top shelves her Heath candy bars.
Daddy smokes Winstons.
Jim buys Lays chips
from his paper route money.

I salivate thinking about
German Chocolate cake
in our dented loaf pan.
A long skinny slice won't be noticed.

Crumbs drop from sticky fingers.
Momma's coming.
I gobble faster than taste buds enjoy.
Cellophane tears but stretches enough.

I wash evidence from my hands.
Momma opens the frig.
She eyes me, feels my guilt.
Liquid is missing from her 7-up bottles.

"I didn't do it, Momma."
She doesn't believe me.
Jim savored my punishment,
and her pop – I'm sure.

I'm never satisfied
with leftovers.
I want more.
I always want more.

Written in 2010,
Honorable Mention in PST March 2012 Contest

Keeping Track of Time

When I worked seven to four
I looked forward to Fridays
signaling the end of long weeks.
I used others' measuring criteria.

Once I told my parents
I anticipated a day off.
Dad laughed, "I don't get a day
off from my retirement."

Mom interjected to him,
"Yes, you do. You just don't
remember which day it is."
Now, I live his joke.

I mark Fridays off my
calendar. My retirement
week isn't regimented any more.
I don't feel a definite ending.

Posted on Poetic Asides *2009*

Keepsake

a Diamante form

Keepsake
Mary's locket
His kiss gave it to her.
They broke up seven years ago.
Her man shouted he never would come back.
To her, that day will always remain black.
Sad, she still feels he was her beau.
That gift stores his picture
in her pocket.
Heartache

1977 Written for DWU Creative Writing class

King of the Moment

I am
Red-Winged Blackbird,
King of my world.
From bottom to top,
all I touch and see
becomes mine
for that moment.
I balance
on fingertips of my tree
to view my salted sky.
I own this moment.
Hear me sing.

2005 published in Schrom Hills Park *chapbook,*
2010 Honorable Mention in the SDSPS contest

Kite Skeleton

The kite, hung precariously
on electric lines, swayed in the breeze.
Childhood skeletons deliver warnings.

March winds labored to loosen it.
A July gust couldn't unbalance the relic.
Spring laughter ended in summer reflection.

Broken dreams may linger.
Thoughts cling as silly toys
hanging on beyond their prime.

1977 Written for DWU Creative Writing class

Lady Jane

a Senryu form

"Tea and prune crumpets
taste dusty on prairie soil,"
Lady Jane bemoaned.

Written in 2011

Lady Like

Ladies
don't need
to be lady-
like.

1977 Written for DWU Creative Writing class

Lamb of God

Did John fully understand the words
and depth of what he said in honor?
Didn't he know of Abraham's words,
God . . . will provide the Lamb. . . offering?   *Gen. 22:8*

Could Moses have really meant Jesus,
when he said, *Slaughter the Passover Lamb?*   *Ex. 12:21*
Isaiah's Lamb silently slaughtered
knew of Christ's passion day.

Revelations of hope for those still
struggling with this miserable life know:
only the slain Lamb can open
the seals of the closed eternal scroll.

Our precious Jesus, the Lamb of God,
was born as full payment for our sins.
John exclaimed, *Look, the Lamb of God,*
who takes away the sin of the world!   *John 1:29*

Christ has been revealed as our own Lamb,
and sacrificed for our salvation.
Help us *wash our robes and make them white*
in the blood of the Lamb, our Jesus.   *Rev. 7:14*

Only then may we stand before the Lamb's throne
and be counted worthy of heaven.
Thanks be unto God and to the Lamb
forever and ever. Amen.

2005 published in Faith and Spirit *chapbook*

Last Minute

Clock-watching will not stop
one year from adjourning
and ticking on to more possibilities.

No celebratory toast propelled us
from the boardroom of yesterday
into the boiler room of a new year.

My strategy stretches far beyond
that one last minute. A new schedule
includes living my best each day.

With a kiss, a wish, and a prayer,
I nodded off. The year's last
midnight moment passed in my sleep.

Written in 2011

Late Arrival

You say, "I'm not a Southerner".
You laugh, "I took too long
to arrive here."

Maybe my roots were jerked
out of the South when
my ancestors moved.
Maybe they were looking
for a better life.

Daddy used to sing,
"We like it here. We're going to stay.
We are too poor to move away."

Did you stay, because
you couldn't move away?
Or did you stay because life truly
was better? Or just familiar?

It took me jobs, education, then a career,
marriages, divorces (yes, multiple of both),
step-kids, children, moves for improvement,
retirement, care-giving, and family deaths.

Now, I'm here and you say I don't belong
or I'm not a true Southerner?
Maybe my ancestors were born in the
South. Maybe their sympathies were
with the South. Maybe they just had
other things to worry about.

What does it matter? Aren't we all
American? I didn't shoot your great-
great Papaw in the big War Between
the States. My Daddy, my Granddaddy,
and three of my Great-granddaddies
didn't participate in any Civil War.

They concerned themselves with survival.
The one who did fight, probably
only needed a job. I doubt he cared
about slavery or the cotton market.

You're not the only one who can remember
living a generation away from outhouses
and depression. You're not the only one
who suffered, because there were no jobs.
My daddy worked on the WPA, the CCC,
and served in World War II.

When will you ever stop seceding?
When will we ever put away
our petty differences and
embrace our similarities.
Let's truly pull together
as Team America.

Posted on Poetic Asides *2009*

Latest Lie

a Dorsimbra form

Swing higher, beyond the sapphire blue sky.
Reach dream clouds shape-shifting across the wind.
Do not think long about his latest lie.
Only remember, it was he who sinned.

Cheating,
breaking vows,
crossing lines,
he lost your trust.

Relax and float free in the pool he built.
Spend his money. Leave none for his next love.
Thank the stars he never gave you children.
Forgive yourself and let him go his way.

Written in 2011

Laundry

Laundry
piles unmercilously
wait for the week-end wash cycle.
It's the last load. I sigh,
"I'm done."

1977 Written for DWU Creative Writing class

Learning Time

Learning time has passed.
I passed! I'm a graduate.
Today, I hold a certificate
saying I need never study again,
not late at night, or
pushing deadlines, pleasing
instructors, stretching my brain.
But I'm a poet;
learning time has just begun.

Written in 1978

Learning Tree

a Concrete or Picture form

Word
upon word
I learned to
read. Picture books began
teaching me words and sentences.
Soon I could read comic books,
History books, English books. Text books taught
me what I needed to know. Novels, essays,
and poems rounded out my education so I would not
need to attend school any more. My education
completed, I was through with learning.
Huh!

1977 Written for DWU Creative Writing class
Published 1978 in Prairie Winds, *Volume XXVIII*
and 1978 in CMA Review

Leavening

No interesting TV
No baking allowed
No one watching

Carol kneaded trouble.
Who would know
she stirred up the dough?

Carol forgot
she buried
failed batch.

Father arrived home.
Rising mess
stuck to his shoes.

Christian camp counselor,
listened to girl's story,
related leaven parable,

told Carol her recipe
didn't fail, but
secretly grew.

She explained God's plan.
His unseen kingdom
also quietly rises.

Written in 2012

Leering Date

a Senyru form

Sue's date slurps pasta,
leers at dessert special. . . Her
spaghetti straps flee.

2010 1ˢᵗ Place April PST monthly contest and
published in Tennessee Voices Anthology 2009-10

Life and Death

Oh, Death, I forgot our appointed date.
I remember nothing before my birth.
My life of joys and sorrows, weren't they great?
I dread this coming time to leave this earth.
When did we agree on my departure?
Perhaps during my sorrow and sadness.
That time seems too long ago and obscure.
Will you cruelly pluck me from happiness?
I've escaped your clutches in my spent youth
middle years, sixty on the horizon.
I've regretted lies and practiced my truth.
How much longer before you say I'm done?
    Time ticks away, no begging for minutes,
    no more than I deserve for my penance.

Written in 2009

Rose Klix

Life is Love

Life
Is

Love

As

Love
Is

Life

Surround

Love
In my

Life

Infuse

Life
In my

Love.

Written in 2008

Life is a Spinning Top

Keep me constant and make me pure.
God's mighty love – my only cure.
My life is like a spinning top.
It goes and goes. When will it stop?

I'm dizzy. Life barely slowed down
to put my feet on dry ground.
Many days I stopped and prayed.
I thanked Jesus for all He paid.

New Year promises unwind.
My sin-filled thoughts refuse to mind.
Christ is come! Yes, He is still here.
The season's drawn Him near all year.

The top's spinning out of control.
Wish I knew when I'd reach my goal.
I can't seem to slow myself down.
My life has been all spun around.

My life is like a spinning top.
It goes and goes. When will it stop?
Keep me constant and make me pure.
God's mighty love, my only cure.

2003 published in The Way of the Cross, 2005 *in* Faith and Spirit *chapbook, and* *2012 in* Common Ground Herald.

Life Not Your Own

Your life isn't your own.
Remember you're not just living
your life. You're sharing
with your husband's life.
He's sharing too.

Your life isn't your own.
What you do isn't just for you.
It's for both of you.
You have a special reason now
to be careful with your life.

Your life isn't your own.
You share in the life that you carry.
You must be even more careful
because what you do doesn't just hurt you.
It hurts that being inside of you.

Written in 1971

Living Lights

Green, Yellow, Red
Go, Wait, Stop
All day long you flash.
Green, Yellow,
Red, Green,
Yellow, Red
Which is it?
Go, Wait, or Stop?
Make up my mind.

Written in 1985

Living on the Economy

Iraklion Air Station, Crete, Greece, 1992-93.

The land of civilization, the initial seat of democracy,
radiated brown dust and olive drabness
mixed with Mediteranean blue.

Greek language lessons only helped me
recognize numbers and days of the week.
Often I confused *kali mera** and *kalamari.***

Our four-plex rental with whitewashed cement blocks
stayed unfinished so the landlord avoided taxes.
Rural blended with urban where sheep grazed our backyard.

A neighbor's butcher shop waited patiently for the lambs.
Island summertime festive party atmosphere, subtitled
movies in open air bars, and rumors of topless beaches.

Few Cretan's owned the old i*sland cars.*
Three-million rented scooters avoided traffic lights,
kilometer limits, and passed on the sidewalk.

I salivate my memories of the chocolate mouse's
sweet shop and gyros from the pita stand,
but I missed lettuce on salads.

A ten-year phone line waiting list prevented Mother calling me.
Occasionally, into the base's pay phone, I shouted to family
across the ocean, often rudely disconnected.

Reliable electricity disappeared when long Egyptian storms
blew winter across the Mediterranean. Wooden shutters
didn't keep the rain and wind from entering paneless windows.

Propane heat struggled to warm our *flokoti**** covered marble
floors and twelve-foot ceilings built for summer tourists. A bidet
sat beside the toilet bowl with too narrow plumbing pipes for tissues.

Unprocessed sea clung to my showered skin, when water
wasn't stolen by tourists for hotel swimming pools.
Vendors selling oranges giggled and patted my cheeks.

Drunken servicemen celebrated the New Year
with a polar bear swim. In the English pub,
I beat them at darts and won $200 in the slot machine.

I loved our visit to Knossos, the Minoan Royal Palace.
In Fodele, we almost visited El Greco's museum,
but who had the key? They would rather sell embroidery.

Our ferry's historic Christmas trip to Athens
sounded dangerous when we heard
street bombs explode nearby.

Crete's nickname *the island of cats*, rang true when
Pork Chop Hill waiters, cried, "Take kitty,"
in their limited English language repertoire.

I experienced my first unisex restroom
where a swinging wooden door separated
the man's stall next to me. No one spoke.

Bob, the scrappy tomcat, begged for tuna outside
the commissary. He gained adoption from a
departing service family when the air station closed.

I looked forward to landing where I enjoyed
more reliable electricity, heat, treated water, and
a telephone. Home, Sweet USA.

*kali mera = good day, good morning
**kalamari = squid
***flokoti = sheepskin rug

Written in 2010 in Jane Hicks Workshop sponsored by PST-NE

Lonely

Lonely is having insomnia
when everyone else is asleep.
Lonely is staying up
to see the late, late, late show
and finding you'd seen it
three times before. You turn
off the sound and learn lip-reading.
Lonely is cleaning house at midnight.
Lonely is trying to get the Great Dane
next door to bite you so you
get to know your neighbors.
Lonely is clipping Mr. Jackson's bushes with a saw.
Lonely is thinking about winking
at a married man so his wife will talk to you.
Lonely thoughts make me pathetic.

Written in 2004

Long Drive

The night is dark chocolate
melting the road
in front of me.

The first greeting
in my hometown
is always a red light.

Written in 2008

Lost

I can't go home
this way. Oh, dear,
now what shall I do?

I like straight lines
and square corners
and now I can't go that way.

You can't lead me.
I need to find
my own way.

Written in 2004

Lost Again

I sit in the far left lane
awaiting the light change
contemplating my next U-turn
To get me back on the right road.

I hate being lost. I shouldn't ever move
from the familiar to the new.

Written in 2011

Love Is . . .

Love is
       being looked up to
       never seasonal
       never lonely
Love is
       respecting
       now and always
       being together
Love is
       giving
       taking
       all this and more

Love is being with you!

Written in 1962

Love Spans a Solid Bridge

I

Love spans a solid bridge
from cliff to rugged crag.
Affection, heritage –
coarse planks which often sag.

Splinters of Trust echo,
chastising weathered cracks.
Painful rotting holes grow
where suspicion ransacks.

II.

Gray content boards crumble,
privately secluded,
spreading Despair's rubble
of expressed love muted.

Concern's clumsy attempt
stumbles on rusted nails.
Apathy meets Contempt,
fracturing blistered rails.

Torched insatiable Wrath
inflames rotting timbers,
transforms the tranquil path
to flickering cinders.

Solitude screams. Confused
echoes span the chasm.
Care surrenders with bruised
Hope's despondent spasm.

IV

Faith covers ugly warts,
kills Despair that murders,
builds confident supports,
cements steel girders.

Trembling, Love, hurry.
Run across our new bridge.
Unconditional, free –
caress the tortured Edge.

Written in 1996, 2007 published in Open Hearth
and 2011 in Images of Love *Anthology by PST-NE*

Love's Triangle

She was who she was, who she wanted to be.
He saw not her, but who he wanted to see.
Then, love was second to none between
Master Joe and his bonnie young Jeanne.

A look, a glance would not stay petite.
They cried that love they could not repeat.
Serving up soup or baking the breads,
Jeanne stopped daydreams and turned down the beds.

Gallop away on your horse now, Lord Joe.
Go kiss Lady Emma. Your love won't grow.
Dancing and feasting away in the night,
don't stop your thinking she loves your birthright.

Married life sat stale as bread in the air.
No one was happy. Now no one would care.
She was who she was, who she wanted to be.
He saw not her, but who he wanted to see.

Written in 2009

Luminosity

Comet, streak across the sky.
Light the Midwest – Coast to Coast,
brilliant, demanding Star.

Decision made – can't turn back.
Mundane doubt is for the meek.
Accept danger and intrigue.

Move on – glow still – hypnotize,
Coasts to Midwest. Live, laugh,
light up the black sky.

Caution thrown – it's been hurled.
Illuminate the darkness.
Today excitement is no crime.

Brilliant, demanding Star,
Light the Midwest – Coast to Coast.
Comet, streak across the sky.

Written in 1988

Macho Farm

My father said –

"If the barn is bigger
than the house,
the man wears
the pants in the family."

If twin silos
tower the barn,
I wonder what it says
about such erect edifices.

2008 published in Barn Charm *chapbook*

Magnolia Blossom

an Acrostic form

Maggie's aunt was a hearty magnolia blossom
As surely as one blooming in her yard.
***G**irls shouldn't climb trees, she giggled.*
***N**o, they might tear their clothes.* She mocked.
***O**h, but birthing babies is sooo easy.* Her eyes rolled.
***L**ord, such a messy business.* Words escaped around her hand.
***I** just wanted one or two, but tried twelve!*
***A**nd don't you know, my arms are still empty.*

Begetting tears, she swallowed memories of
Lingering bitter pills. She smiled and touched
Our hands with cold tremors. Releasing nameless
Someones, drop by drop as dripping molasses.
Steel blue eyes cleared. Visiting time evaporated.
One kiss bruised her wrinkled cheek. Even wax
Magnolia blossoms fade away to memory and
So did Wilma Clarmont's eighty-eight years.

Written in 2009

Magnolia Memory

You linger like perfume
from twin magnolia blossoms
we stopped to inhale
one hot, hazy, humid June day.
My closed eyes see you
outlined in my memory,
as surely as staring at sunlight
to blink its captive reflection
into my own darkness.
We are slivers of the same tree.
Thus, you will always be part of me.

2005 published in Schrom Hills Park *chapbook and* *2011* Images of Love *anthology*

Massage Music

pounding brain waves
welcome
massage table's
strong grounding

eases back tension
arching floating
spirit releasing
ascending ego free

flute notes dangling
guitar strings support
my visualized
tropical crystal path

drumming dancing
quarter notes flowing
smoothing sporadic rhythm
skipping through imaginary forest

muscle manipulator's
chimes wake me
respite this time
scheduled again next time

Written in 2008,
Published in Tennessee Voices *2011-12*

Matchmaker

He, an experienced Diddle Web Pressman,
cannot stop to answer questions.
Deadlines drive him
like a whip lashing a horse.
No time off for playing or romance.
Even business telephone calls
make him cranky. No vacation plans.
He's only interested in the backward
and forward motions of the press. He inhales
the stink of ink messages on rolled paper.

She, an entry-level world-wide-web,
virtual map creator, imagines
traveling places she plans for clients.
Playing on the Internet, her virtual dreams
include a relationship of mutual enjoyment.
Her ethereal thoughts melt like sugar lumps.
Loneliness leads her to consider an ad.
The Mollucan Cockatoo was described
as needing lots of attention.
But it costs fifteen-hundred dollars.

Mutual friend arranges a meeting.

He agrees to Starbucks for black coffee,
only to stop the friend's nagging.
Going Dutch sounds especially fair.
He insists his fifteen-minute break sufficient.

She decides the public meeting place
a pleasant idea. A leisurely cup of latte
sounds delicious. Conversation should be
more interesting than with a needy bird.

Who knows? Sometimes opposites attract.

Written in 2004

Mc Barn

M marks Exit 13,
high on the hill
guarding the barn
waiting for me still.

2008 published in Barn Charm *chapbook*

Medicine

Medicine is getting way out of hand.
It costs more than it's worth, including
side effects, upon side effects.
Really. Listen to any ad.
Remind me again,
why medicine is good for me.
Or is it good for the pharmacy?

Written in 2010

Middle of a Muddle

West of the east coast and
east of the west coast
the Midwest is in the middle of a muddle.
Maybe if Lewis and Clark paddled canoes
west to east, it would be called the Mideast.
Too confusing, given world politics.

The top of the west coast is the Northwest,
but Oregon and Washington are still
considered the west coast. Idaho and
Montana are in the Pacific Northwest, but
part of the Midwest. Arizona and New Mexico
are the Southwest, but are in Mountain time
like some Midwest states.

Twelve states are all definitely Midwest.
Even though some are Great Lake states
and a few survived the Old West.

Then there's the east coast and its subdivisions.
The Northeast, the Southeast and the Midatlantic.
Whew! With all these lines drawn it's not clear.

Many states should be obvious,
but can also be something else,
like Florida in the Southeast of the east coast,
and Texas in both the Southwest and Gulf Coast.
How do we include Alaska and Hawaii?

I've got us into the middle of a muddle,
just wondering about the Midwest,
why it isn't also the Mideast.

Sometimes, the lines are quite blurred.
At least we're all American in the United States.
But, what about Washington, DC
and the territories? They're not even states.

Oh, my head is full so I'll just quit traveling
with my mind and go find some regional food.
But which region am I hungry for?
Forget it. Ethnic food might be easier.

Written in 2003

Momma's Quilts

You left me quilts and quilts.
You'd finished all you could,
stuffing the batting with yards
of my wonderful memories.

I shared your work with others.
A children's hospital loves your
Scrappy Scarecrow design.
Boys and Toys comforts an abusive refuge.
A raffled sampler bought wheelchairs.

I saved my favorites, gave to family
and friends, sold to appreciative fans,
donated leftover supplies and your
rainbow fabric stash to a quilting club.

You taught me how to piece color
and shape my own uniqueness.
I inherited your craft but
adapted it for my own existence.

I chose to piece together words,
shape them into patterns,
animate them with senses,
and type them on this page.

Written in 2009

Morning Glory

Early walks are best to find,
morning glories smiling bright.
They welcome gentle dew
and grin at first winks of light.

Today is a tentative time to be a tender vine.
Does she unintentionally choke while she clings
to spiral planned bushes? I feel she fears
independence. So, she hugs other things.

One blossom gazed skyward before
the gardener jerked the weed by the root.
His orders said to pull it up
and out from underfoot.

I cried for a thing of beauty
but too late to save the unappreciated guest.
Often seeds planted by God
are not wanted where they are happiest.

Written in 2007

Morning Prayer

Thank you, Lord God, eternal light,
for our safe passage through the night.
Thank you for your constant might.
Guide our feet this day
to tread on right paths on our way.
In Jesus name we pray. Amen

Written in 2001

Morning Scramble

a Pirouette form

Sun's up and so are you
shining mirror bright as
a scrubbed aluminum
biscuit pan cooking up

a warning, *Good Morning.*
A Warning? *Good Morning?*

Close the drapes keep out the
sunshine. Shut up the birds.
Leave me alone for now.
Grouch awake. Be alert!

Written in 2009

Mortuary

I stopped into a morgue today
to bless those who'd passed away.
The man greeted me with a smile
and beckoned me to stay awhile.

I slowly came in and closed the door.
I think I saw blood on the floor.
I held back, but he gave my hand a jerk.
Come on now. I want you to see my work.

He wasn't angry, 'though perhaps a little mad.
I told myself, *Go on now. It can't be that bad.*
He led me into another room.
It looked like it hadn't seen a broom.

Bodies were lying on several tables.
They were only held on by cables.
He drew me closer and tried to explain,
but all I could see was the terrible pain.

A youth lay over there in a corner.
He had a hot car and loved to roar her.
Pieces of glass, lay all around him.
As of yet, they hadn't embalmed him.

A young girl lay completely undressed.
Her hands were folded across her young breast.
The man thought sadly of her lying in her coffin.
He said, *It's a pity she died a virgin.*

A dog by a young boy lay.
Then, the horrid man did say,
After this dog ran the little boy,
all in pursuit of a silly toy.

There were many more people he described to me,
but not one more sufferer could I stand to see.
I ran out of the morgue crying
Why do they keep on dying?

Then I awoke with such a start
to hear the beating of my heart.

Written in 1968

Mother's Box

Mother was an odd-sized box
who once seemed to work better
vertically with paintbrushes,
quilting needles, and romance novels
than horizontally with pills.

When transparent, she led girls
to try new experiences whether
primitive camping in Yellowstone
or selling Girl Scout cookies.
Many leaders learned from her.

Her quilt shop taught thousands
to embrace color and create their own
beautiful quilted family heirlooms.
Her foundations continue in local
and state guilds and quilt shows.

Her very soul was trapped inside.
Few were allowed to see her fully open.
She was rather like the festival puzzle boxes
with fancy carving. Difficult to tell where
they would slide open and for whom.

She gaped frequently for strangers.
For me, she opened only a crevice.
Oh, but the precious treasures
she held inside were priceless
jewels of wisdom I mine deeply now.

One day a vaporous spirit escaped
from her box. I tried to capture it.
She wouldn't allow me to hold her.
She floated away leaving me here
to question our relationship and myself.

Written in 2004

Mother's Good-Bye

Viet Nam is so far away.
Just for me, will you please pray?

Jimmie, my little boy,
your gun is not a toy.

God tells us not to kill.
Thou shalt not. . . but you will.

War, such an ugly senseless game,
I wish that letter never came.

Each and every night, for you, I'll pray.
You must go. You better leave today.

Please come back and don't die.
Good-bye, Jimmie, good-bye.

Written in 1966 after my brother was drafted

Mouse Orates Hymn

a Haiku form on Thomas Eakins painting
titled The Pathetic Song, 1881
(defeated singer – judgmental pianist and apathetic old man)

Mouse orates her hymn,
squeals in latticed crocus wings,
deafens ignorance.

Written in 2009 at Abingdon's Creative Writing Day
with Carolyn Kreiter-Foronda, Poet Laureate of Virginia
2012 Honorable Mention in National League of American Penwomen Cape Cod
Chapter Haiku contest and 2012 published in Penwoman magazine.

Ms Muffet

a Nursery Rhyme Parody

Little Ms Muffet
sat down to tough it.
She couldn't eat her whey.
That troublesome spider,
why wouldn't he shy her?
He's squashed now and thrown away.

1988 2nd Place South Dakota State Fair, Huron, South Dakota and
1989 1st Place Central States Fair, Rapid City, South Dakota

Musica, Dei Donum

Clashing cymbals roar
with Zeus's thunder.
Flutes whisper frolic
in Pan's playful winds.

Music
crescendos emotions,
soothes lonesome moments,
celebrates familial traditions.

Music
fills silences,
quiets meditation,
translates thoughts.

Violins whine love's sorrow
from Venus's heartbeats.
Trumpets rejoice and announce
victory of Mars, god of war.

Music
rhythms rhyme our reality,
understands sensory paths,
creates understandings of unity.

Music
dances my soul free,
releases pain,
reaches others.

Written in 2009

My Faith

Sometimes,
my faith is a frayed thread.
Sometimes,
it's a strong flossing string.

Many times,
my faith is lost in church.
Many times,
I find it by an unpolluted stream.

Any time,
my faith is in my soul speaking my truth.
Any time,
my faith is laughing and crying with my Deity.

Published on FanStory.com *in 2009*

My Office the Day After I Died

after Patrick Phillips poem – *In the Museum of Your Last Day*

You filled a trash can with all my scraps,
prompts, file folders,
my few printed publications.

My computer hard drives were ripped
from my laptop and bagged with
the week's potato peels and tomato tops.

You stripped the bookcase
of my reference books
and packed them for Goodwill.

My empty desk sits outside
waiting for Frontier Industries
to pick up cast-off donations.

You might keep the office chair
to sit at the window and wonder
why you can't remember me.

Written in 2011

My Philosophy of Life

I lived the best I knew how.
Every line was an ad-lib.
There are a lot of actions I should put in
the out-takes video for the trash.

Life, in general, is a constant recycling,
a regeneration of the ancient
into the contemporary fascinated
with the antique.

I loved so many people, one at a time.
Once in a while, I let them know me.
My neighbors generally weren't
the difficult ones to love.

Whatever is Chihuahua puppy
fresh for this generation is mature
bloodhound on the porch
for the previous ones.

I learned much from my mistakes and
believe I'll take a chance in a new life.
Oh, I hope I can carry some
knowledge with me.

My life was a research project.
I lived; I loved; I learned.
That's my epitaph.

Written in 2005. Published on FanStory.com in 2008

No, no, no! Wait!
Don't stop reading yet.
Volume II continues with poems titled from N-Z

A comprehensive list of Acknowledgements,
a chronological listing of when the poems were
written and a concordance of themes are also
in the back of Volume II.

About the Author

I am what I learned, from whom, but I am responsible for how I applied that knowledge. Rose Klix

Rose earned her *cum laude* Bachelor of Arts degree in English with an emphasis on Creative Writing from Dakota Wesleyan University, Mitchell, South Dakota in 1978. This allowed her to practice poetry in a prescribed setting.

Her family roots go deep in South Dakota. "From my paternal grandparents I inherited a pioneering spirit. My grandfather **John Frederick "Fred" Rose** died when Dad was a toddler. He used his mechanical and carpentry skills homesteading on the prairie. Perhaps I inherited his pursuit of a variety within my writing craft – 'a jack of all trades and a master of none.' My grandmother **Gertrude Grace (Olmstead) Rose** showed me endurance during difficult times. I inherited *1000 Beautiful Things*, a book compiled by Marjorie Barrows.

My maternal grandmother **Jennie Grace (DeGeest) Swinehart** showed me patience with love, self-sufficiency and beautiful embroidery. My impatient grandpa **Orion Wyant Swinehart** demonstrated love with a clever sense of humor. He expressed art through his pen and ink drawings, tumbled stones, and his miniature western towns made from sticks. I've recently discovered he'd written volumes of short stories, that I'm now enjoying."

Rose was transplanted a number of times, but always managed to connect with fellow poets and writers, as is demonstrated on her Acknowledgement pages in Volume II.

Rose's website is http://www.RoseKlix.com

Made in the USA
Columbia, SC
12 July 2018